BOSTON

**WHAT TO DO, WHERE TO GO, AND
HOW TO HAVE FUN IN BOSTON**

by Helen Byers

John Muir Publications

Santa Fe, New Mexico

John Muir Publications,
P.O. Box 613, Santa Fe, NM 87504

Printed in the United States of America
First edition. First printing September 1997
ISBN: 1-56261-363-4

Editors Peg Goldstein, Krista Lyons-Gould
Graphics Jane Susan MacCarter, Steve Dietz
Production Janine Lehmann, Nikki Rooker
Cover Design Caroline Van Remortel
Typesetting Diane Rigoli
Illustrations Caroline Van Remortel
Maps Susan Harrison
Activities Peg Goldstein, Bobi Martin
Printer HiLiter Graphics/Burton & Mayer
Cover Photo Leo de Wys Inc./Vladpans
Back Cover Photo © Marjorie Nichols

Distributed to the book trade by
Publishers Group West
Emeryville, California

*While the author and publisher have
made every effort to provide
accurate, up-to-date information,
they accept no responsibility for loss,
injury, or inconvenience sustained by
any person using this book.*

About the Author
Helen Byers has written and illustrated several
books for young readers. She has also edited
literature and textbooks for adults and children.
She lives in Massachusetts.

CONTENTS

〜〜〜〜〜〜〜〜〜〜〜〜〜〜〜〜〜

1/ Welcome to Beantown! 1

2/ Historic Sites and Landmarks 14

3/ Historic Sites Out of Town 48

4/ Parks and the Outdoors 60

5/ Good Sports 74

6/ Museums and More 84

7/ On the Town 102

Calendar of Events 114

Resource Guide: When, What,
and Where? 118

Answers to Puzzles 127

Geographical Index: Where Is Everything? 132

Index 133

COLOR THE ROUTE
FROM YOUR HOMETOWN TO BOSTON

If you're flying, color the states you'll fly over. If you're driving,
color the states you'll drive through. If you live in
Boston or Massachusetts, color the states you have visited.

WELCOME TO BEANTOWN!

BOSTON IS ONE OF THE GREAT AMERICAN CITIES. It's full of surprises and things you can't find anywhere else. It has buildings, roads, and cemeteries that were old before the United States even became a country. Boston's history is special because it's where people *began* making the country.

But Boston is also a modern city, where native New Englanders and people from all over the world live side by side. It has great music, exciting sports, zany street performers, delicious food, thrilling museums, peaceful parks, stuff to buy, and more wonders than you'll ever have time to discover!

On a map, Boston looks like the hub, or center, of a wrecked bike wheel. The biggest roads—circling Boston—look like the tire. The roads going into town look like broken spokes.

⬆ **Located on the Atlantic Ocean and the Charles River, Boston is surrounded by water.**

NAMES AND NICKNAMES

In the beginning, Boston wasn't called Boston. Native Americans called it *Shawmut* because it had springs and waters full of fish. In the Indians' language, Shawmut meant "living waters" or "living fountains."

Then English settlers came. They called their new home Boston, after a port city in England.

Of all Boston's nicknames, "the Hub" may be easiest to remember, because of how the city looks on a map. But the people of Boston would never think of themselves as the center of a wrecked bike wheel! They believe their city is the hub of New England—and the universe!

Boston has been called "the Athens of America." Like Athens, the capital of ancient Greece, it's a great center of education and the arts.

Boston is also known as "the Bay City," because it's located on a bay—in the "Bay State," Massachusetts.

And, of course, Boston is "Beantown," famous for its baked beans!

⇑ The "Bay City"

THE PILGRIMS

The history of Boston includes the earliest history of the United States. The first English settlers, called Pilgrims, came to Massachusetts in 1620, more than 150 years before the United States was a country. They made colonies in Plymouth, Gloucester, and Salem. In 1630, on a piece of land surrounded by a river and a bay, one group made a colony that they named Boston.

⇧ **An artist's view of what the Pilgrims' landing at Plymouth might have looked like.**

The Pilgrims were Puritans who had left England so they could be free to practice their religion. But the Puritans themselves didn't welcome other religious beliefs. In fact, during the 1650s,

the Puritans forced one religious group, the Quakers, to leave Boston. Some Quakers who returned were punished or executed.

In those days, many people were superstitious. In 1692 in Salem, 150 people were put in jail, 19 were hanged, and one was crushed to death—on charges that they were witches.

COLOR THE SCENE

The *Mayflower* carried the Pilgrims to America in 1620. Today you can go aboard the *Mayflower II* when you visit Plymouth near Boston.

TEA AND TAXES

In 1765 more than 15,000 colonists lived in Boston. They were still British citizens. But now that they were living in North America, they didn't want to pay taxes to Great Britain. The British government thought of New England as a colony that belonged to old England. So, in 1768, British soldiers arrived to make sure the colonists in Boston did pay their taxes.

By 1773 colonists had formed the Sons of Liberty, a group that resisted British rule. One night, the Sons of Liberty climbed aboard three British ships loaded with tea. They threw the tea into the harbor to show that they refused to pay taxes on it. That was the Boston Tea Party. It led to the Revolutionary War.

⬆ **Angry colonists dressed as Indians and boarded British ships.**

REVOLUTION

On the night of April 18, 1775, two express riders for the Sons of Liberty, Paul Revere and William Dawes, galloped on horseback from Boston toward Concord. They went different ways, stopping at every house to warn people that British "regulars" (soldiers) were on their way to take the colonists' hidden weapons in Concord.

At dawn the next morning, the first battles between the British and the Minutemen (the colonists' army) happened in Lexington and Concord. The Battle of Bunker Hill followed two months later. An army led by George Washington finally drove the 10,000 remaining British out of

↗
Paul Revere's ride

Boston on March 28, 1776. That year, the Declaration of Independence was first read here.

During the late 1700s, Boston became an important seaport. Merchants prospered from shipping. They shipped goods from India, Asia, and the East Indies to Boston—and from Boston around the world.

If you haven't read Henry Wadsworth Longfellow's poem "The Midnight Ride of Paul Revere," you can get a copy in the gift shop of Old North Church.

GROWING UP

The 1800s were a time of big changes in Boston. By 1800 about 25,000 people lived here. But by 1850 there were 137,000 people—nearly six times as many. Thousands came from Ireland, Italy, Portugal, and Eastern Europe, hoping to find a better life. But Boston didn't have enough room for all these new Bostonians. So the city leaders decided to make more space. They flattened two of the city's three hills and used all that earth to fill in part of the river! They added another 60 feet of dirt, scraped off the top of Beacon Hill. Boston built new houses on this landfill. The neighborhood's name is Back Bay.

During the rest of the 1800s, Boston attracted writers, artists, teachers, and scientists. It also attracted merchants, railroad builders, bankers, insurance agents, and cloth makers.

⬆ **Boston rooftops looked like this in 1871.**

BOSTON TODAY

Today more than half a million people live in Boston "proper"—the main part of the city. The Greater Boston Area includes nearly 3 million people, living in 90 cities and towns. Greater Boston has 56 colleges and universities. It has become a center of education, medicine, music, finance, and computer technology. The Pilgrims would never recognize it!

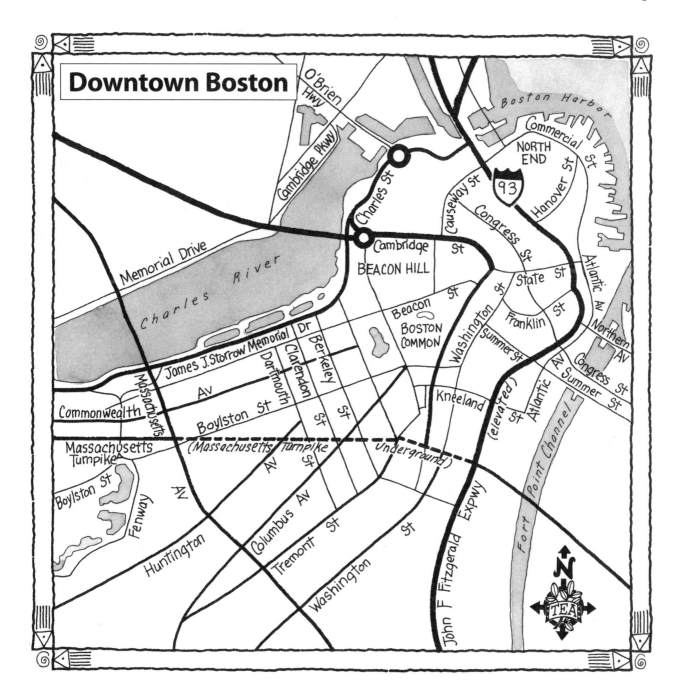

Downtown Boston

FIRST AND OLDEST THINGS

Boston has lots of "oldest" things in the country. For example, it has the oldest lighthouse, the oldest subway, the oldest public park (Boston Common), the oldest African American church building, the oldest university (Harvard), the oldest marathon, the oldest public library, the oldest college library (Harvard), and the oldest public school (Boston Latin).

Many things also happened first in Boston. Boston had the first newspaper in America, published in 1690. Boston was the first American city to create city parks.

⬆ **Boston's green trolleys, the first subway line, began in 1897.**

It had the first railroad. It was the first American city to say how tall new buildings could be. It sent the first African American regiment to fight for the Union in the Civil War.

WHAT?

People in Boston have a special way of doing certain things. Talking, for example. Bostonians don't pronounce their *r*'s.

People might tell you that Bostonians say, "Pahk the cah in Hahvud Yahd." But they don't really say that. No one tries to park even near Harvard Yard these days. Parking spaces are too hard to find!

But Bostonians do say "Hahvud Yahd." They say "Ahlington" when they

⇧ **The Gloucester fishermen's memorial faces out to sea.**

⇧ **Harvard Yard is the oldest part of Harvard University.**

mean Arlington. They say "Concud" for Concord, "Glostah" for Gloucester, "Medfud" for Medford, and "noth" for north. They also say "Peab'dy" for Peabody and "Quinzee" for Quincy.

The first Bostonians came from England, so they spoke with British accents. Later, people came to Boston from other countries, with other accents. Over time, English in Boston began to sound like English no place else.

WEATHER AND WHAT TO WEAR

There's a saying about the weather: If you don't like it, wait. It will change!

The weather changes a lot in Boston. In the spring plants bloom and might make you sneeze. In summer, it can be hot and humid. Fall is the best time, because it's cool and the leaves turn colors. Winter can be fun or not fun—depending on how much snow or ice there is (and what you're trying to do in it).

Because Boston is by the sea, it often cools down at night. So dress for the

⇧ **Lights forecast the weather on top of the old Hancock building.**

season. Wear cool clothes in summer. Wear a jacket, mittens, and hat in winter. Pay attention to the forecast, and plan ahead. And don't forget your sneakers!

For the forecast, Bostonians find the tower of lights on the old Hancock building and recite this old rhyme:

Steady blue—clear view.
Flashing blue—clouds due.
Steady red—rain ahead.
Flashing red—snow instead.

What's the forecast today?

GETTING AROUND

Boston is crazy to drive in. Even Bostonians hate driving here. Drivers shout and honk. There are too many of them. There's no place to park! They pass on the right. They pass in the breakdown lane! They speed. They don't act grown up. But it's not all their fault. Boston was never built for cars.

Luckily, you can walk most places here. Or take the subway, called the Ⓣ. MBTA buses travel throughout the Boston area. Trains and buses travel between Boston and other parts of Massachusetts. Ferries and other boats take people to Charlestown, Gloucester, the Harbor Islands, Cape Cod, and Martha's Vineyard.

⬆ **You can see the town from a horse-drawn carriage.**

Within Boston, there are also tour buses and trolleys. One tour bus even floats on water. It drives you around Boston, then into the Charles River, then back onto land! In summer, there are horse-drawn carriages in downtown Boston. There are guided and self-guided walking tours. Boston for Little Feet and Make Way for Ducklings are guided walking tours just for kids.

> **At a bookstore, you can buy a copy of *Car-Free in Boston*. It's full of tips on getting around here.**

2 HISTORIC SITES AND LANDMARKS

BOSTON HAS MORE LANDMARKS AND historic sites than some towns have buildings! The tallest skyscraper is the John Hancock Building. There's Old North Church, remembered for the warning lanterns in its white steeple the night of April 18, 1775. There's the State House, with its golden dome. There's Fenway Park, the old baseball park. There's Chinatown Gate, with four marble fu dogs that protect the neighborhood. There's even a giant milk bottle!

Many sites are along the historic Freedom Trail and the Black Heritage Trail. These walking paths go through parts of Boston that remind us of struggles for freedom before and after the American Revolution.

↥ In Copley Square, Trinity Church looks small beside modern skyscrapers.

 On July 21, 1997, the USS *Constitution*, a famous Boston warship, celebrated its 200th birthday. As part of the celebration, the ship set sail in Massachusetts Bay.

Custom House tower has four clocks.

BEFORE YOU EXPLORE

Visit the information booth on **Boston Common** or the **Greater Boston Convention & Visitors Bureau** for tourist information and maps. Ask about special discounts and hotel deals for kids and families.

At Copley Square, find the **John Hancock Building**—the tallest building in New England. It's a huge mirror, reflecting the sky. Take the elevator to the 60th floor. Here you get an eagle's view of the city.

Can you see the State House, with the golden dome, or the Custom House tower, with the clocks? Try using a telescope.

There are special exhibits here. "Boston 1775" is a multimedia show. "Skyline Boston" shows how the city has changed. "Aviation Radio" lets you listen in on conversations between planes and Logan Airport's control tower! Before you leave, test what you've learned about Boston on one of the computers here. Now it's time to explore.

The John Hancock Building is the tallest of all.

HISTORIC BOSTON

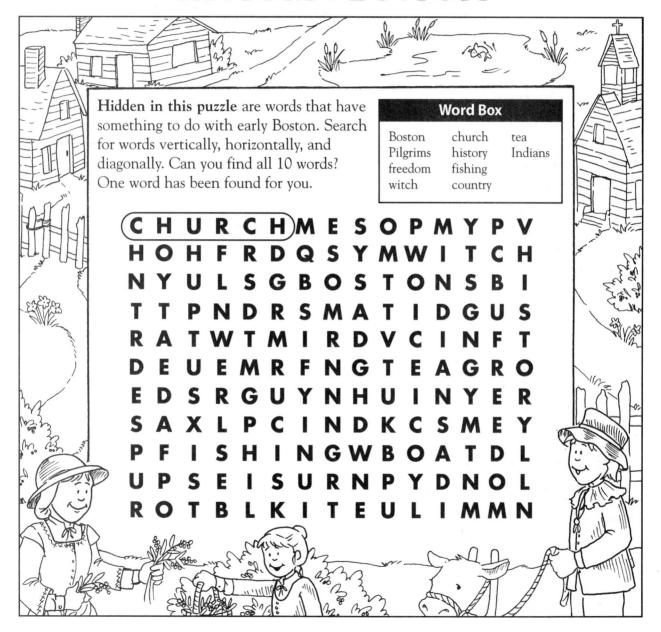

Hidden in this puzzle are words that have something to do with early Boston. Search for words vertically, horizontally, and diagonally. Can you find all 10 words? One word has been found for you.

Word Box

Boston	church	tea
Pilgrims	history	Indians
freedom	fishing	
witch	country	

```
(C H U R C H) M E S O P M Y P V
 H O H F R D Q S Y M W I T C H
 N Y U L S G B O S T O N S B I
 T T P N D R S M A T I D G U S
 R A T W T M I R D V C I N F T
 D E U E M R F N G T E A G R O
 E D S R G U Y N H U I N Y E R
 S A X L P C I N D K C S M E Y
 P F I S H I N G W B O A T D L
 U P S E I S U R N P Y D N O L
 R O T B L K I T E U L I M M N
```

BEACON HILL

Beacon Hill is where Boston's first English settler—William Blackstone—built a cottage and grew an orchard in the early 1600s.

In the 1800s, many wealthy Bostonians lived on Beacon Hill. The neighborhood looks almost the same today. The streets have gas lamps. The big brick houses have shutters and fancy iron fences. As you walk along Pinkney, Mt. Vernon, and Chestnut Streets, try to imagine the sounds of the past. In those days, there were horse-drawn carriages and pushcarts, with peddlers selling food door-to-door.

If you play detective, you'll find boot scrapers, hand railings (for walking on icy sidewalks), and old horse stables. Acorn Street is paved with stones from the Charles River. Louisa May Alcott, who wrote *Little Women*, lived at 10 Louisburg Square.

⬆ Beacon Hill

Beacon Hill got its name in 1634. A bucket of tar was put on top of the hill, to be set on fire as a beacon, or warning light. It was never used.

WHAT'S THE DIFFERENCE?

These two pictures of old Beacon Hill might look the same, but they're not. Can you find at least 14 differences between the two drawings?

THE BLACK HERITAGE TRAIL

The first African Americans in Boston were slaves brought by English settlers in 1638. But by 1790, all Massachusetts citizens were free.

In the 1800s, many black Bostonians lived on the north side of Beacon Hill. The Black Heritage Trail is a walking tour past 14 sites there. It is marked with signs on lampposts.

The trail begins at the **Robert Gould Shaw and 54th Regiment Memorial**, across from the State House. The memorial reminds us of the first black soldiers, and their white officer, who fought with the northern states in the Civil War. At the **Lewis Hayden House**, escaped slaves found a hiding place on the Underground Railroad. The **African Meeting House** is the oldest black church building in the United States.

You can go inside the African Meeting House and the **Abiel Smith School** and **Museum of Afro-American History**.

⬆ Memorial to the 54th Massachusetts Regiment

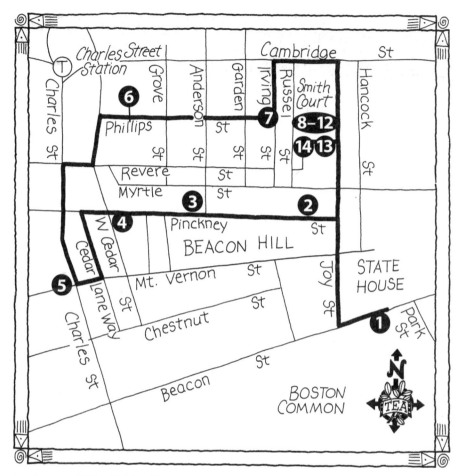

The Black Heritage Trail

❶ **Shaw and 54th Regiment Memorial** (Beacon and Park Streets, Boston Common)

❷ **George Middleton House** (5–7 Pinckney Street)

❸ **Phillips School** (Anderson and Pinckney Streets)

❹ **John J. Smith House** (66 Phillips Street)

❺ **Charles Street Meeting House** (Mt. Vernon and Charles Streets)

❻ **Lewis Hayden House** (66 Phillips Street)

❼ **Coburn's Gaming House** (2 Phillips Street)

8–12 **Smith Court Residences** (310 Smith Court)

⓭ **Abiel Smith School** (46 Joy Street)

⓮ **African Meeting House** (8 Smith Court)

FREEDOM TRAIL AND BOSTON COMMON

The Freedom Trail travels 3 miles from Boston to Charlestown. The path is marked by a red brick or painted red line. You can start walking anywhere along the trail. (You're free to choose!) But Boston Common is a good choice.

Boston Common is the oldest park in the nation. In 1634 sheep and cattle grazed here. It was also a place of punishments. From the Great Elm tree (now gone), the Puritans hanged pirates, thieves, Quakers, and people they called witches! Later, soldiers were trained on Boston Common. Horses were raced. There were fireworks, concerts, and speeches.

People still love to use the Common. They make music and do magic tricks. They eat pretzels. They take naps on the lawn. In winter, they ice skate on **Frog Pond**.

⬆ Founders' Monument on Boston Common

On the Beacon Street side of the Common, the Founders' Monument shows Boston's Pilgrim colonists meeting William Blackstone, the first settler. He sold them this land.

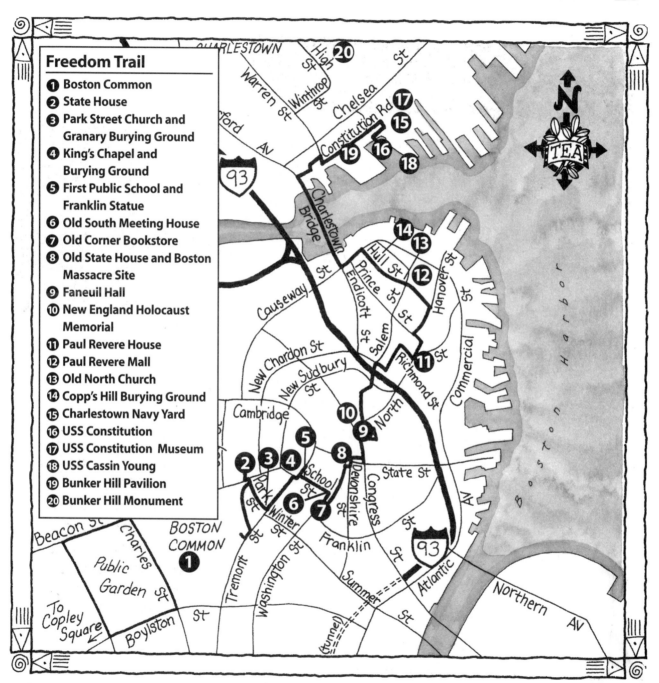

Freedom Trail

1. Boston Common
2. State House
3. Park Street Church and Granary Burying Ground
4. King's Chapel and Burying Ground
5. First Public School and Franklin Statue
6. Old South Meeting House
7. Old Corner Bookstore
8. Old State House and Boston Massacre Site
9. Faneuil Hall
10. New England Holocaust Memorial
11. Paul Revere House
12. Paul Revere Mall
13. Old North Church
14. Copp's Hill Burying Ground
15. Charlestown Navy Yard
16. USS Constitution
17. USS Constitution Museum
18. USS Cassin Young
19. Bunker Hill Pavilion
20. Bunker Hill Monument

THE STATE HOUSE

The State House is the capitol of the Massachusetts Commonwealth. It's where the state's business is done.

The building was designed by a famous architect, Charles Bulfinch. Samuel Adams laid the cornerstone on July 4, 1795. In 1798 the finished dome was covered in copper given by Paul Revere. Today the dome is covered in gold.

Outside are statues of two women from Boston's Puritan colony. Anne Hutchinson was forced to leave the colony because her religious beliefs were different. Mary Dyer, a Quaker, protested the colony's punishment of people with different beliefs. She was hanged from the Great Elm tree.

Inside, you can visit the house and senate chambers and watch the state government in session. You can visit the Hall of Flags and study portraits of Massachusetts governors.

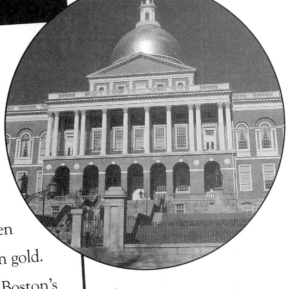

⬆ The State House dome gleams in the sun.

What's that huge fish dangling from the house gallery ceiling? It's the Sacred Cod, a reminder of an important Massachusetts industry—fishing. Today, cod are scarce. Can you guess why?

Freedom Trail Site

COLOR THE PICTURE

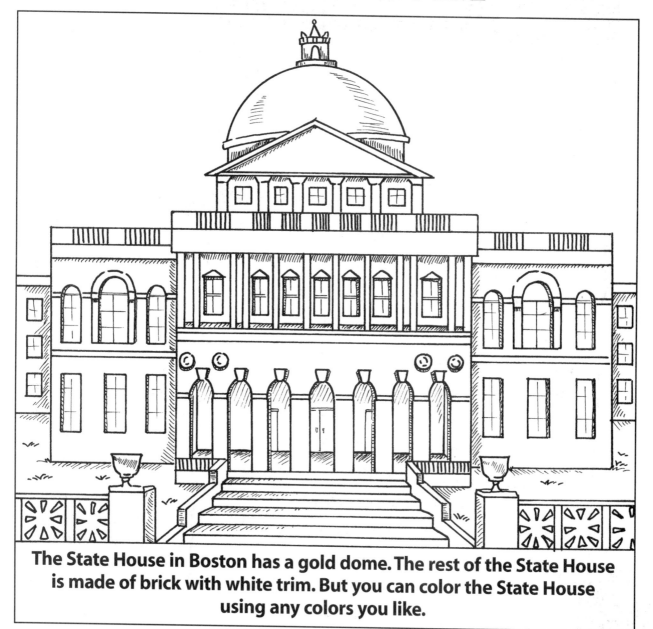

The State House in Boston has a gold dome. The rest of the State House is made of brick with white trim. But you can color the State House using any colors you like.

PARK STREET CHURCH

Park Street Church sits on the corner of Park and Tremont Streets. This was once called Brimstone Corner because brimstone (gunpowder) was stored inside during the War of 1812. Also, "hellfire and brimstone" preachers gave speeches outside. Speeches were given in the church, too. William Lloyd Garrison, an important abolitionist, gave his first speech against slavery here in 1829.

"My Country 'Tis of Thee" was first sung at Park Street Church, in 1831. Everyone already knew the tune. It was the British song "God Save the King." But no American would sing *those* words anymore!

Freedom Trail Site

🌲 **Park Street Church on "Brimstone Corner"**

A NEW ANTHEM!

Write a new national anthem in the space above, using the tune to "My Country 'Tis of Thee."

GRANARY BURYING GROUND

⬆ **An obelisk marks the grave of Benjamin Franklin's parents.**

Freedom Trail Site

Granary Burying Ground has been here since 1660. People buried in it include signers of the Declaration of Independence—John Hancock, Samuel Adams, and Robert Treat Paine—plus Paul Revere and Benjamin Franklin's parents.

Hunt for the grave of Mary Goose. She was called Mother Goose because she and Isaac Goose had ten children. After Mary died, Isaac married Elizabeth. Elizabeth Goose raised Mary's children—plus ten of her own! It was the second Mother Goose who made up rhymes for all those children. But no one knows where *she's* buried.

Certain words look funny on the old gravestones. People wrote differently hundreds of years ago. Stone carvers shortened words. They wrote *Ss* like *Fs*. They used spellings that aren't right today. Some words had different meanings then. The word *ye* meant "the" as well as "you." See how many gravestones you can read.

CONNECT THE DOTS

**Connect the dots to finish the drawing of Mother Goose's grave.
Then color the picture.**

King's Chapel burial ground is the oldest in Boston.

KING'S CHAPEL

King's Chapel may look odd from outside. That's because it never got a steeple. The church was first built in 1688. A newer building was constructed in 1754. As the name hints, this was the first Church of England in Massachusetts. After the Revolution it became the first Unitarian church in America.

You can sit in the box pews. In colonial times, families owned these pews and sat in them during *very* long services. People who didn't pay attention got poked with a long pole by someone called the beadle! The pews were shaped like boxes to keep heat in. People brought little coal burners to church to warm their feet in cold weather.

Why doesn't the church have stained glass windows? Because members didn't want fancy things in their church. The King's Chapel bell, like many other bells in Boston, was made by Paul Revere.

⇧ **Spooky old gravestones in King's Chapel burial ground were carved by hand.**

Freedom Trail Site

CROSSWORD FUN

There is a lot to discover about American history in Boston. Solve this crossword by figuring out the clues or completing the sentences. Write your answers in the boxes, going either across or down. If you need help, use the clue box.

Clue Box

bells
church
coal
England
Massachusetts
pews
Puritan
steeple

Across

2. People rang _____ to mark the time in colonial days.

4. Chapel is another name for a _____.

5. Churchgoers sat in _____.

6. Boston's first settlers came from _____.

8. Boston's first settlers belonged to this religious group.

Down

1. There's no _____ on King's Chapel.

3. Boston is part of this New England state.

7. In colonial days, people burned this to keep warm.

FIRST PUBLIC SCHOOL SITE AND FRANKLIN STATUE

🔥 **Born in Boston, Ben Franklin is honored here.**

Freedom Trail Sites

Walking along School Street, you will come to the site of the first public school in the country, Boston Latin, built in 1635. Don't walk too fast! A mosaic, a kind of picture, in the sidewalk marks the spot. The mosaic, *City Carpet*, was made in 1983 by Lilli Ann Killen Rosenberg. Bits of glass, brass, and pottery spell out the names of famous students, including Benjamin Franklin, John Hancock, and Samuel Adams. Can you name every picture in the mosaic alphabet? Boston Latin School still exists. And guess what. Its students still study Latin!

Beside the old City Hall, the Franklin Statue is a bronze sculpture of Benjamin Franklin. Boston calls him a Bostonian—even though he ran away to Philadelphia when he was 17. The base of the statue shows pictures of things Franklin did as a scientist, printer, patriot, and peacemaker.

WORD SCRAMBLE

Unscramble the letters to find out where you can find
Benjamin Franklin's picture.

rendhud

_____

lodlra

_____

lbli

_____

Clue: You might have to go to a bank to find one of these.

OLD SOUTH MEETING HOUSE AND OLD CORNER BOOKSTORE

↑ **Old South Meeting House**

Freedom Trail Sites

Old South Meeting House was built in 1729 as a Puritan church. But it's best known as the site of town meetings just before the American Revolution. A famous meeting was held the night of the Boston Tea Party—December 16, 1773. Afterward, angry patriots, wearing "war paint" for disguise, snuck down to the harbor. They boarded three British ships loaded with tea—and tossed it in the water. They refused to pay taxes on the tea.

Inside Old South, you can listen to audio programs on headphones. To hear what was said here on the night of the Boston Tea Party, listen at pews 2 and 3.

Across the street, the Old Corner Bookstore has been used as a printer's shop, home, and apothecary's shop (drugstore). During the 1800s, books by Boston authors—including Nathaniel Hawthorne, Henry Wadsworth Longfellow, and Harriet Beecher Stowe—were published here.

HIDDEN MESSAGE

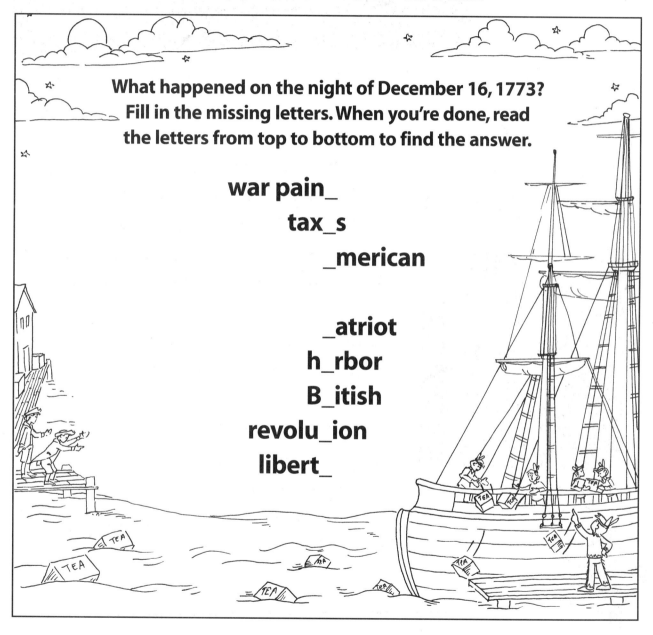

What happened on the night of December 16, 1773?
Fill in the missing letters. When you're done, read
the letters from top to bottom to find the answer.

war pain_

tax_s

_merican

_atriot

h_rbor

B_itish

revolu_ion

libert_

OLD STATE HOUSE AND BOSTON MASSACRE SITE

The Old State House, built in 1713, is the oldest public building in Boston. It was used at the same time by the British government and the Massachusetts Assembly. The Declaration of Independence was first read from the balcony, on July 18, 1776. The crowd went wild! They destroyed the lion and the unicorn—symbols of Great Britain. (The eagle on the other end of the building stands for America.) The lion and the unicorn weren't replaced for 100 years.

Below the balcony (in the traffic island) a ring of cobblestones marks the Boston Massacre Site. On March 5, 1770, a scuffle broke out between some colonists and British soldiers. One soldier, or "redcoat," was knocked down. His musket went off. The other redcoats fired into the crowd, killing five men. One was Crispus Attucks, the first African American to die as a patriot.

⬆ **The Old State House looks tiny today.**

The Declaration of Independence has been read from the Old State House balcony every Fourth of July since 1776.

Freedom Trail Sites

COLOR TO FIND THE ANSWER

British soldiers had a nickname. Color numbers 1–3 using gold. Color numbers 4–6 using black. Color numbers 7–9 using red. Color numbers 10–12 using pink, tan, or brown. Color numbers 13–15 using white. Color the areas with letters using any color you like. When you're done, guess the nickname for the British soldiers.

FANEUIL HALL

Faneuil Hall overlooks Faneuil Hall Marketplace — also called Quincy Market. When Faneuil Hall was built in 1761, this area looked different. The harbor shore was nearby. Ships were loaded and unloaded on the docks. Faneuil Hall had stalls where merchants sold meats, vegetables, and dairy goods. Upstairs, colonists gave fiery speeches about freedom and independence. That's why Faneuil Hall was nicknamed "The Cradle of Liberty."

From Faneuil Hall, the Freedom Trail leads to Boston's **North End**. (Remember to follow the red line.) On your way, explore the very old area between Union and Blackstone Streets.

Stop on the island between Union and Congress Streets to explore the **New England Holocaust Memorial**, a monument to six million Jews and others who were killed by the Nazis in World War II. Read the words and numbers, and look closely above and below as you pass through the six glass towers. What does the memorial say to you?

↑ **Merchant Peter Faneuil built Faneuil Hall in 1761.**

In Boston, "Faneuil" rhymes with "flannel."

Freedom Trail Site

LEAPING LETTERS!

How many words can you make from letters in the word
FANEUIL? Two words have been found for you.
How many more can you find?

FANEUIL

Nail _____   _____   _____

Fun _____   _____   _____

_____   _____   _____

_____   _____   _____

_____   _____   _____

PAUL REVERE HOUSE

Paul Revere—silversmith, bell maker, Son of Liberty, dad—may be the most famous Bostonian of all. The night of April 18, 1775, he was rowed secretly across the harbor, under the guns of a British ship. Then he galloped a horse from Charlestown to Lexington to warn the colonists that British soldiers were coming to take their weapons.

⬆ **Paul Revere's house**

The Paul Revere House, built in 1680, was already old when Revere and his family, including 16 children, lived here from 1770 to 1800. In the 1800s, when many immigrants moved to the North End, landlords turned the house into tiny apartments. Today, it's the oldest building in Boston. You can see Revere family belongings and samples of Paul Revere's metalwork. Read Revere's stories of his adventure on April 18!

Nearby is **Paul Revere Mall**—a small park with a statue of Revere on his "midnight ride."

Paul Revere was an express rider for the Sons of Liberty. He once rode on horseback from Boston to Philadelphia in five days. Every Patriot's Day, a modern "Paul Revere" rides again from Charlestown to Lexington. But not as fast!

Freedom Trail Site

A MIDNIGHT RIDE

Without telling what you're doing, ask someone for a word to fill in each blank. For example, say, "Give me an action word." When all the blanks are filled in, read the story out loud. One of the blanks has been filled in for you.

Carlos and his sister Ana __jump__ed through the park. "Hey, there's the
_____ (action word)

_____ of Paul Revere on his _____ midnight ride," said Carlos.
(object) .... (describing word)

"He must have been very _____ to ride at night with no
.... (emotion)

streetlights," said Ana.

"Someday I'm going to take a midnight ride," announced Carlos.

"I don't think so," said Ana. "We're not allowed outside after _____
.... (number)

o'clock."

Late that night a _____ _____ woke Ana up. Carlos was
.... (describing word) (sound)

talking in his sleep. "The British are coming!" he yelled.

Well," Ana giggled, "I guess Carlos is taking his

midnight ride after all."

OLD NORTH CHURCH AND COPP'S HILL BURYING GROUND

Christ Church is the oldest church in Boston. It was built in 1723. It's called "Old North."

Old North was important on the night of April 18, 1775. In the church's steeple, the sexton, Robert Newman, raised two lanterns as a signal. They warned Paul Revere that the British were taking a shortcut from Boston—crossing the "back bay" by boat—rather than marching all the way to Concord.

When he was 12, Revere rang the bells of Old North. George Washington worshipped here when he visited Boston. His friend, General Lafayette of France, said the bust of Washington inside the church looked just like him.

Copp's Hill Burying Ground has been a cemetery since 1660. British soldiers gathered here for the Battle of Bunker Hill. Can you find the headstones they used for target practice?

↥ **Old North Church overlooks Paul Revere Mall.**

Old North's eight bells are still rung every Sunday at 12:15 p.m. On the third Monday night every April, two lanterns shine again in the steeple.

Freedom Trail Sites

SEND A SIGNAL

Send a secret signal to Paul Revere. Draw lights in the steeple of Old North Church. Then color the picture.

USS CONSTITUTION

From Copp's Hill, the Freedom Trail takes you across the **Charlestown Bridge** to **Charlestown Navy Yard**.

Here you'll climb aboard a sailing vessel launched in 1797. It's the USS *Constitution*, known as "Old Ironsides." It's the oldest warship still afloat in the world.

⬆ **You can go aboard Old Ironsides.**

As the crew, dressed in costumes, will explain, the sides of Old Ironsides aren't really made of iron. They're oak. But the frigate got its nickname during the War of 1812. Cannonballs from the British fleet just bounced off the wood!

The **USS Constitution Museum** can teach you more about Old Ironsides. On an interactive video program, you can become a crew member during the War of 1812.

Also at Charlestown Navy Yard, you can board the World War II destroyer **USS *Cassin Young***.

Freedom Trail Site

ALL ABOARD

"Old Ironsides" is sitting in the harbor. Draw your own boat beside it. Then give your boat a name.

BUNKER HILL MONUMENT

The Battle of Bunker Hill, on June 17, 1775, was the first big battle of the Revolutionary War. Colonists were low on ammunition. So an officer ordered, "Don't shoot until you see the whites of their eyes!" The tactic worked. More than 1,000 British soldiers were killed or wounded. The colonists lost 441. Yet the British claimed victory. Who do you think won the battle?

At the **Bunker Hill Pavilion,** near the Charlestown Navy Yard, you can watch a half-hour reenactment of the battle in a wrap-around theater. The multimedia show is narrated by "Paul Revere."

On top of the hill, the Bunker Hill Monument offers a spectacular view of Boston. That is, if you climb all 294 steps to the top of the 221-foot-high monument!

Freedom Trail Site

⬆ **Bunker Hill Monument (in background) on Breed's Hill**

The Battle of Bunker Hill was a scene of terrible suffering for the injured and dying soldiers. In 1775 Boston didn't have a hospital!

MY TRAVEL JOURNAL
—Historic Sites and Landmarks—

I had fun when I visited: _____

I learned about: _____

What I enjoyed the most was: _____

This is a picture of what I saw in Boston

3 HISTORIC SITES OUT OF TOWN

ANY TOUR OF BOSTON'S HISTORIC SITES should include the towns of Lexington and Concord, half an hour away, where the Revolutionary War began. Another interesting town is Salem, made famous by witch trials, sea captains, and the author Nathaniel Hawthorne.

Within an hour of Boston, in Plymouth and Sturbridge, there are living history museums, where actors dressed as villagers help you imagine what life was like hundreds of years ago. Historical parks and heritage parks, such as the one in Lowell, invite you to have fun while learning about the past.

⬆ **Plimoth Plantation is a living history village.**

The Pilgrims landed first at Provincetown, on Cape Cod. They arrived at Plymouth Rock later.

LEXINGTON

In Lexington, the **Museum of Our National Heritage** and the **Lexington Visitor Center** have exhibits and information. The **Battle Road Visitor Center** (part of **Minute Man National Historical Park**) has films about the events of April 19, 1775.

Sites to see include the **Hancock-Clarke House**, where Paul Revere woke up John Hancock and Samuel Adams. As Revere galloped past at midnight, alarming every home, a sentry asked him not to make so much noise. "Noise?" Revere yelled. "You'll have more noise than this before long! The regulars are coming out!"

At **Buckman Tavern**, 77 Minutemen waited for the redcoats. On **Lexington Battle Green**, the first musket shots were fired. **Monroe Tavern** was used by the redcoats as a field hospital.

If you visit Boston on Patriot's Day, look out for redcoats.

Every third Monday in April is Patriot's Day. Starting at 5 a.m. in Lexington, actors dressed as Minutemen and redcoats act out what happened that morning in 1775!

HELP PAUL REVERE!

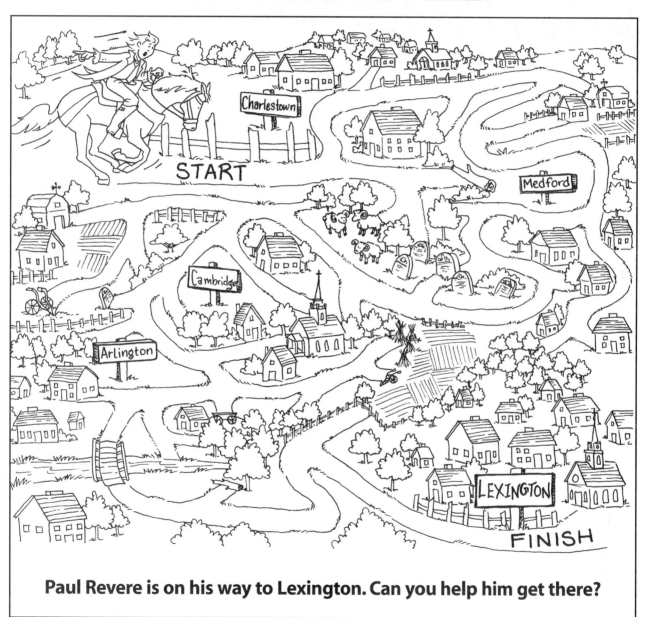

Paul Revere is on his way to Lexington. Can you help him get there?

CONCORD

Like Lexington, Concord is proud of its history and its many old houses. First, stop at the **Concord Visitor Center** to get a map and information. Then visit the **North Bridge Visitor Center** (also in Minute Man National Historical Park) to see exhibits and a model of old Concord. Rangers will describe the second battle between Minutemen and redcoats at the **Old North Bridge**. The meadow by the Old North Bridge is a nice picnic spot. Visit **Concord Museum** to examine one of the lanterns Robert Newman raised in the steeple of Old North Church.

In the 1900s, Concord's famous writers included Louisa May Alcott, Nathaniel Hawthorne, and Ralph Waldo Emerson. You can visit their houses. Nearby is **Walden Pond**, where Henry David Thoreau built a tiny cabin and wrote about nature.

Actors re-create the battle at Old North Bridge.

Nathaniel Hawthorne rented Concord's Old Manse, a large house, from 1842 to 1845. The cost was $100 per year. He thought that was expensive.

UNSCRAMBLE THE WORDS

Unscramble each word and match it to the picture of something you might see on a visit to Concord, Massachusetts.

grdebi _____

tneanlr _____

hchruc _____

ehuso _____

SALEM

Salem, just north of Boston, is a city full of history. Do you love boats and ships? During the 1700s, Salem became an important port. The **Salem Maritime National Historic Site** has exhibits all about early Salem. The **Peabody Museum** also has exhibits on maritime history, and on natural history.

Salem is also the place where the terrible witch trials and executions of 1692 took place. The **Salem Witch Museum** has a short play of the witch trials. At the **Witch Dungeon Museum**, a scary jail helps you imagine how accused "witches" were treated.

In nearby Danvers, you can visit the **Rebecca Nurse Homestead**. Rebecca Nurse was one of the Salem women accused of being a witch.

↥ **Lifelike models tell the story at the Salem Witch Museum.**

In Salem you can visit The House of the Seven Gables, author Nathaniel Hawthorne's birthplace. Have you read his book with that name?

WHICH WITCH?

Hidden in this puzzle are words that have something to do with the Salem witch trials. Search for words vertically, horizontally, and diagonally. Can you find all 10 words? One word has been found for you.

Word Box

witch	Salem	craft
punish	dungeon	trial
fear	spooky	
crime	judge	

```
W O Z A T K M E S O P M J D V U H
H I H F R D Q S Y S H E U A O N H
N Y T L S G A B N A P K D D N T F
T T P C D R S K A L G N G U L U D
R A T R H M N R D E C E E B E D N
D E U I M D F N P M N I N T Y E Y
E D S M G P U N I S H J R Q T W R
S B F E A R I N D K C L M R R D W
P O N D U K R S W B J A T F I Q T
U I S E I S U R N P Y D C R A F T
S P O O K Y I T E U L I M Y L F S
D Y D N I O P Y D U N G E O N Q R
```

PLYMOUTH

From April through November, you can visit **Plimoth Plantation**, a living history museum near the modern town of Plymouth. It includes **Pilgrim Village** and **Hobbamock's Homesite**. At Pilgrim Village you'll see how the Pilgrims lived in 1627. You'll see copies of their gardens and thatched homes, talk with actors dressed as Pilgrims, and watch them do their chores. At Hobbamock's Homesite, you can meet Native Americans whose Wampanoag ancestors met the Pilgrims. They will show you their traditional ways of cooking, farming, making a canoe, weaving, and making pottery.

In Plymouth, visit **Plymouth Rock**, where the *Mayflower*, the Pilgrims' boat, landed. Then go aboard the *Mayflower II*, which crossed the Atlantic Ocean from England more than 300 years later. (The crew pretends today's date is 1620. They're about to sail back to England!)

⇡ **Plimoth Plantation**

Plymouth is in cranberry country. Visit Cranberry World (Ocean Spray's free museum) to learn all about this native American berry. Then taste some free samples.

MIXED-UP PICTURE STORY

The Pilgrims came to America on the *Mayflower*. Put the scenes in the correct order by writing a number in the bottom left-hand corner of each picture.

STURBRIDGE

An hour west of Boston, **Old Sturbridge Village** is another living history museum. Here, on 200 acres with meadows, woods, gardens, 40 buildings, and a working farm, you can visit a Massachusetts country village from the 1830s.

You'll get to meet the costumed "villagers" and their animals. You can watch the villagers work at their many crafts—including pottery making, shoe making, tin working, blacksmithing, farming, wool spinning, weaving, and quilting. You might even get to help!

Special events happen at Old Sturbridge at different times of year. You might share an old-fashioned New England Thanksgiving dinner or ride in a horse-drawn sleigh (if there's snow).

Allow plenty of time for your visit here, since the village and grounds are so big.

⇡ **Life was different in the 1830s. At Old Sturbridge Village you'll learn how children worked and played in those days.**

MY TRAVEL JOURNAL
—Historic Sites Out of Town—

I had fun when I visited: _____

I learned about: _____

_____

My favorite site was: _____

This is a picture of something I saw • • • • •

PARKS AND THE OUTDOORS

WHETHER IT'S ANIMALS YOU WANT TO SEE or a sport you want to play, Boston has all kinds. You can see whales in the ocean, gorillas at the zoo, and painted turtles in a wildlife park. You can make sand castles or sit on huge rocks at the beach. You can pick apples or pumpkins. You can be a park ranger for a day!

Boston has open spaces for everyone. It has nearby beaches and islands. There are meadows and woods for walking and hiking. There are ponds and rivers for canoeing and sailing. Indoors or outdoors, you'll discover the nature of New England.

⬆ **Vip, a mature lowland gorilla, lives in the Franklin Park Zoo.**

NEW HAMPSHIRE
MASSACHUSETTS

Lawrence

Gloucester

Lowell

Peabody
Salem

Concord

Lexington

Lynn

Lincoln

Cambridge

Atlantic
Ocean

BOSTON

❶

Framingham

Quincy

Weymouth

Brockton

Provincetown

Cape Cod
National
Seashore

Wellfleet

❷

Plymouth

Providence

Wareham

Sandwich

Dennis

Bourne

Fall River

Hyannis

New Bedford

Falmouth

Woods Hole

Oak Bluffs

Nantucket
Sound

Newport

Edgartown

❹

Martha's
Vineyard

Nantucket

❺

Nantucket
Island

e Island
Sound

**Nature and the
Outdoors around
Boston**

❶ **Boston Harbor Islands**
❷ **Cape Cod**
❸ **Emerald Necklace
City Parks**
❹ **Martha's Vineyard**
❺ **Nantucket**
❻ **Stone Zoo**

CITY PARKS

Boston has a string of nine parks, called the Emerald Necklace, that stretches from **Boston Common** to **Franklin Park**. Boston Common is the first "emerald." The second is the **Public Garden.** Swan Boats have paddled the pond in the garden since 1877. Hop on! You can also feed the ducks, study the statues, or look at flowers. Other "emeralds" include the **Arnold Arboretum** (with thousands of trees to run or picnic under) and **Jamaica Pond**, where you can boat or fish.

The **Esplanade** along the Charles River is a place to throw a Frisbee or play on a jungle gym. To rent a boat on the Charles, go to **Community Boating. Waterfront Park** overlooks Boston Harbor.

↑ **You can ride Swan Boats past real swans at the Public Garden.**

Robert McCloskey's *Make Way for Ducklings* is a story about a duck family that decided to move to the Public Garden from Beacon Hill. Read the book, then find their statues in the park!

PARTY IN PUBLIC GARDEN

Without telling what you're doing, ask someone for a word to fill in each blank. For example, say, "Give me an action word." When all the blanks are filled in, read the story out loud. One of the blanks has been filled in for you.

Eric called his friend Beth on the phone. "Can you come to a party at the Public Garden?" he asked.

"That sounds like fun," said Beth.

"We'll meet at the Swan Boats at ___**noon**___," said Eric.
                                      time

When Beth arrived she was _____ing a big bag of popcorn.
                           action word

"Mmmm," said Eric, "that smells _____."
                                describing word

Everyone who came brought something to eat. They set their food

on the _____ lawn and _____ed to ride the boats. When
       describing word   action word

they came back, _____ ducks were eating the last of their food.
                number

"Uh-oh," said Eric. "Someone forgot to tell the ducks this was a

_____ party."
describing word

THE ISLANDS

Boston's closest islands are the **Boston Harbor Islands**. You can get to them by boat or "water taxi." Explore an old fort, have a picnic, and breathe some salty air!

Park rangers lead tours on many of the islands. On **Little Brewster Island,** you can climb 76 steps and two ladders to the top of **Boston Light,** the oldest lighthouse in America (1716). It's the only staffed lighthouse in the country.

Martha's Vineyard and **Nantucket** are islands off Cape Cod. Depending on the season, you can reach them by ferry from Boston or Cape Cod. Call the ferry offices for reservations. In summer the islands are too crowded for cars. It's easier to walk or rent bikes.

⇑ **Sunset on Martha's Vineyard**

Boston Light can be seen by ships 27 miles out at sea.

HELP LIGHT THE LAMP!

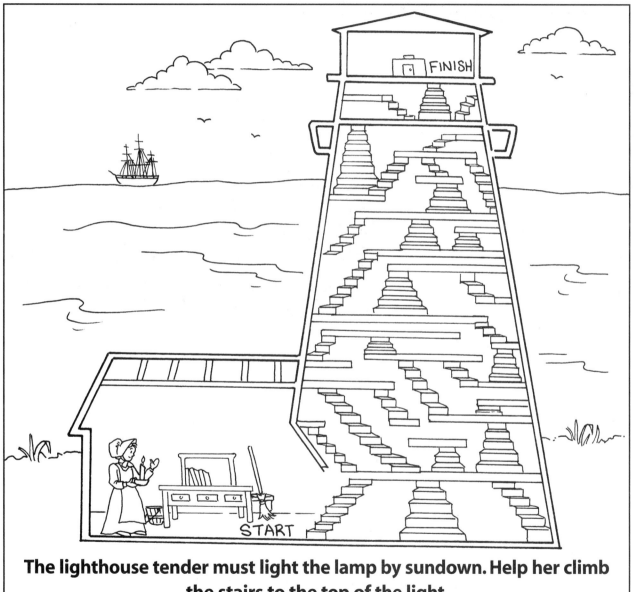

The lighthouse tender must light the lamp by sundown. Help her climb the stairs to the top of the light.

CAPE COD

Cape Cod is a place Bostonians go for peace and quiet. In summer it's mobbed. But there's always nature there.

Stop in East Sandwich to visit the **Green Briar Nature Center**. It has a marsh with a boardwalk that people rebuilt—plank by plank—after a hurricane. The **Cape Cod National Seashore** has beaches, ponds, bogs, dunes, forests, and sandbars. At **Nickerson State Park**, you can get information about the 25-mile **Cape Cod Rail Trail**, where you can run or bicycle between Dennis and Wellfleet. At Woods Hole, visit the **National Marine Fisheries Service Aquarium**.

To learn about day camps, contact the Wellfleet Bay Wildlife Sanctuary, the Cape Cod Association of Children's Camps, or the Cape Cod YMCA.

⇡ **This lighthouse has guided sailors to Cape Cod.**

What's a cape? (Not Superman's kind!) It's land shaped like an arm, flexing into the ocean.

CONNECT THE DOTS

8
7
10 9
5 6 12
11
4 14 ATLANTIC
OCEAN
3
13
15 17
16 18
22 20 19
24 21
23
25 26
28 27
29
BOSTON 30
31
33
32 34
35 36
37 39
38 40
41
1 68
61 60
63 62 59
66
67 64 55 54
65 57 56
58 NANTUCKET SOUND

Massachusetts

Cape Cod
50 51
48 47 52
49 46
45
42
44 53
43

Connect the dots to make your own map of Massachusetts and Boston. When you're done, draw more pictures to decorate the map.

FRANKLIN PARK ZOO

Aren't bongos drums? How wild is a wildebeest? How little is a lemur? How quick is a chameleon? You'll know, once you've been here.

Franklin Park Zoo is in Franklin Park, the 527-acre "crowning jewel" in the Emerald Necklace. In Boston—with its cold winters and hot summers—it's hard to give exotic animals a "natural" habitat. So Boston has made the **African Tropical Forest**, an indoor home for more than 250 African animals and 3,000 plants. Your hair will friz when you enter the big pavilion! You'll see lowland gorillas, pygmy hippos, dwarf crocodiles, and giant lizards. There are big, tiny, and strange birds, all gliding and perching in the vines and treetops. Bring binoculars, if you have them. Some birds are hiding in the jungle.

See a snow leopard

In Stoneham, Stone Zoo has North and South American grasslands exhibits and one of the biggest indoor aviaries (bird exhibits) in the country.

HIDE AND SEEK!

Draw circles around all 12 animals hidden in this drawing. Look for an elephant, little bird, big bird, bear, mouse, hippo, alligator, iguana, monkey, snake, turtle, and gorilla. When you're done, color the picture.

WHALE WATCHING

↥ **If you're lucky you will see a whale—or the flukes of a whale.**

Suppose you're in a boat at sea. Suddenly, a huge shadow passes underneath. Then a gigantic creature—bigger than the boat—comes out of the water right in front of you! What do you do?

You may get to find out. The waters near Boston are feeding grounds for whales. In the past, people killed whales here. They killed so many thousands, that some kinds of whales are gone forever. But, luckily, humpback whales may still be here when you are.

Whale-watching boats leave **New England Aquarium** from April through October. Naturalists will teach you about the sea life here. They can show you the boat's whale-finding radar and radios.

Other whale-watching boats leave from Boston Harbor, Gloucester, Salem, Newburyport, Plymouth, Provincetown, and Nantucket. For information, check the *Boston Globe's* Thursday Calendar, or ask the Greater Boston Convention & Visitors Bureau.

LOOK OUT BELOW

Whales and fishes live in the ocean near Boston. Draw some more sea creatures in the water. Use your imagination!

NEW ENGLAND AQUARIUM

It might be the most awesome thing you've ever seen. The **Giant Ocean Tank** at the New England Aquarium rises from the floor to the ceiling. It holds 187,000 gallons of seawater. Giant sea turtles, sharks, hundreds of bright fish, and a huge coral reef are inside. Would you like to be a diver, feeding every animal in there?

At other tanks and exhibits, you might ask: How fast are those penguins? Am I as electric as that eel? How bright is that flashlight fish?

The **Rivers of the Americas Gallery** invites you to compare two rivers—the Amazon and the Connecticut. Meet an anaconda, a huge snake!

At the **Thinking Gallery**, you can feel the railings to tell the water temperature. An exhibit about Boston Harbor lets you study an example of water pollution.

At the **Discovery Pavilion**, sea lions put on a show. Get splashed!

⬆ **The Giant Ocean Tank might be your favorite.**

MY TRAVEL JOURNAL
—Parks and the Outdoors—

I had fun when I visited: _____

I learned about: _____

_____

My favorite animal was: _____

This is a picture of an animal I saw

5 GOOD SPORTS

BOSTON LOVES TO PLAY! ITS PROFESSIONAL teams are the Red Sox (baseball), Celtics (basketball), and Bruins (ice hockey). It also has dozens of college and school teams.

Some sporting events here are world famous. The Boston Marathon has been run every April for more than 100 years. The Head of the Charles Regatta is a boat race held every October on the Charles River. The U.S. Pro Tennis Championships happen here. The FleetCenter hosts pro basketball and hockey games, as well as World Wrestling competitions and special events such as the U.S. Gymnastics Olympic Trials (1996).

But in Boston you can do more than watch. You can play, too!

⇡ The best long-distance runners and wheelchair racers in the world compete in the Boston Marathon.

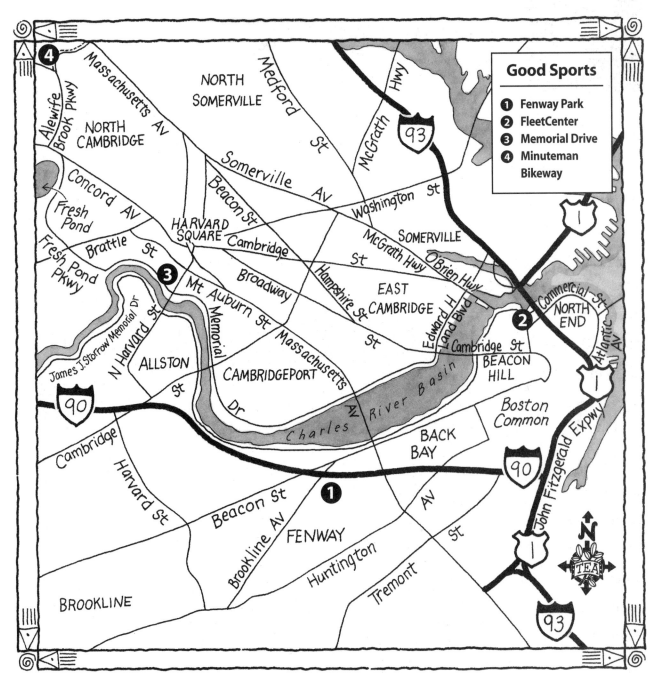

Good Sports

1. Fenway Park
2. FleetCenter
3. Memorial Drive
4. Minuteman Bikeway

BOSTON RED SOX

The Boston Red Sox have been playing baseball since 1901—the first year of the American League. But they've only been called the Red Sox since 1907. First they were the Boston Americans (nicknamed "the Pilgrims" and "the Somersets"). Today people call them "the Sox."

If you go to a Red Sox game, be prepared to meet a monster. The Green Monster, that is! Fenway Park, where the Red Sox play, was built in 1912. It's one of the oldest ballparks in the country. Its walls have odd shapes. They come together at odd angles. The Green Monster is the oddest wall of all. It turns fly balls into homers. It knocks deep line drives back toward the infield. It drives everyone crazy! But no one would change it for anything.

⬆ **Tim Wakefield** pitches for the Red Sox.

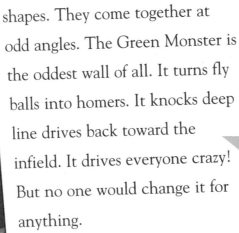

⬅ **It's a hit!**

On May 17, 1947, a seagull dropped a 3-pound fish on the pitcher's mound during a Red Sox–Browns game.

CROSSWORD FUN

You'll learn a lot about baseball at a Red Sox game. Solve this crossword by figuring out the clues or completing the sentences. Write your answers in the puzzle, going across or down. If you need help, use the clue box.

Across

1. This food is a favorite at baseball games.
3. Hitters need a _____ to play baseball.
4. When a player hits a _____ _____, he goes around all the bases.
5. This kind of weather can ruin a baseball game.

Down

2. This player throws to the batter and the catcher.
3. This object is small, round, and white.
6. The "_____ Monster" is really a special wall in Fenway Park.
7. Each team gets three _____ during an inning.

Clue Box

ball	popcorn
bat	outs
pitcher	rain
home run	Green

BOSTON CELTICS

The Boston Celtics have played more than 50 seasons of basketball. They've won almost 1,000 more games than they've lost. But whether the Celtics are winning or losing, Boston loves the whole team.

Some Celtics, like former players Larry Bird and Bill Walton, are super athletes. Bird was the NBA's most valuable player three years in a row (1983–86). Walton was elected to the Basketball Hall of Fame.

The FleetCenter's parquet (paneled) wood floor is almost as famous as Fenway Park's Green Monster. It has 247 panels. Each panel is 5 feet square and $1\frac{1}{2}$ inches thick. The panels are held together by planks, screws, and 988 bolts. When a skating event is planned, a crew called the Bull Gang takes the floor apart. Below it is an ice rink! Putting the panels back together takes $2\frac{1}{2}$ hours.

⬆ **Celtic Antoine Walker**

⬅ **David Wesley goes for the basket.**

PLAY BALL!

It's game time, but the players are missing things. Draw a line
from the athlete to the matching piece of equipment.

BOSTON BRUINS

Do you love the fast pace of hockey? Are your eyes quick enough to see the puck as it skids past the goalie into the net? Do you like to sit right near the rink? Do you stare with your mouth open, wondering how anyone could ice skate as well as those guys?

Bruins versus Whalers

Boston's hockey team, the Bruins, also plays at the FleetCenter. Out come the fans. And up comes the parquet floor!

When Charles F. Adams became owner of Boston's hockey team, he wanted to give it a name that would suggest something big, strong, fast, fierce, cunning, and—brown. Finally, the word *Bruin* was chosen as the team's name. Can you guess what it means? It means "bear." In Dutch it means "brown."

MIX-UP ON ICE

These two hockey games might look the same, but they're not.
How many differences between the two pictures can you find?
Hint: There are at least 13 differences.

SPORTS FOR YOU

What sports will *you* play in Boston?

Most of the year, you can canoe or sail on the Charles River. On the riverbanks, you can walk, run, roller-skate, or fly a kite. On Sundays, part of **Memorial Drive** in Cambridge is reserved for roller skating. For swimming, there are nearby ponds, pools, and ocean beaches. Bicycle paths include the **Minuteman Bikeway** (Cambridge to Lexington and Bedford) and the paths along the Emerald Necklace.

In cold weather, you can ice skate on ponds, including those in the Public Garden and on Boston Common. You can cross-country ski on golf courses, conservation lands, and bicycle paths. Out of town, good downhill ski slopes include **Wachusett Mountain** and others.

⬆ **The beach isn't far away.**

Don't skate on ponds if it hasn't been cold for very long. The ice might not be thick enough. Ask at ice skate rental shops to find out if the ice is safe.

MY TRAVEL JOURNAL
—Good Sports—

I had fun when I visited: _____

I learned about: _____

My favorite sport is: _____

I like it because: _____

This is a picture of something I saw

6 MUSEUMS AND MORE

BOSTON IS ONE PLACE WHERE YOU DON'T have to fret that there aren't enough museums. (You probably were worrying about that, weren't you?) There are nearly as many museums here as there are places to eat! It's no surprise, in "the Athens of America."

But don't assume Boston's museums are just for grown-ups. For one thing, there are lots of kids here—and lots of kids coming to visit. That means Boston has made some museums just for you. And many adult museums have special events or activities for kids. Some of them are so much fun, your parents might want to tag along!

Electricity zaps through an exhibit at the Museum of Science.

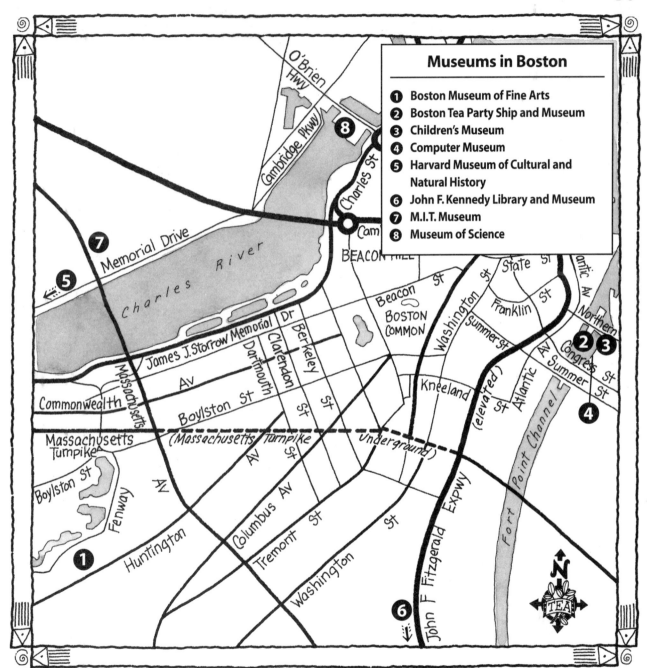

Museums in Boston

1. Boston Museum of Fine Arts
2. Boston Tea Party Ship and Museum
3. Children's Museum
4. Computer Museum
5. Harvard Museum of Cultural and Natural History
6. John F. Kennedy Library and Museum
7. M.I.T. Museum
8. Museum of Science

CHILDREN'S MUSEUM

At the Children's Museum, you don't just look at the exhibits. You get involved with them. The museum teaches you about art, culture, science, and technology. But you might not know it. You might be having too much fun.

You can play on top of a giant's desk. Skipper a boat. Build your own bridge. Take off your shoes and step into a real house from Kyoto, Japan. Play with toys from the past. Compare Kachina dolls made by the Hopi people. You can act in a play. Weave on a big loom. Go to a Latin American *mercado* (market). Sing karaoke— as loud as you want! Make a Japanese *manga* (comic book).

⇡ **The exhibits are kid-size at the Children's Museum.**

⇡ **You can build a house.**

Outside the Children's Museum is a giant, 40-foot-tall milk bottle. If it were real it would hold 50,000 gallons of milk. Instead, you can buy snacks from it.

MAKE YOUR OWN COMIC BOOK

Kids are in the art museum. Can you imagine what they're saying?
Write words in the bubbles to make your own comic book.

COMPUTER MUSEUM

Can a robot make a sandwich? How do computers know your language? What were the first computers like? In this museum, you'll find out.

Maybe you'd like to meet the real R2-D2 from *Star Wars*. It's here. Want to design your own robot? Make a commercial and star in it? Create computer art? You can. You can play on the biggest keyboard in the world. Or "surf the Net." Or race a virtual reality sportscar. Or visit a virtual hospital and see if you'd like to be a doctor. You can track all the planes flying in the sky right now.

At the **Best Software for Kids Gallery**, you can try out CD-ROMs on art, reading, games, science, geography, math, and history.

⬆ **The Computer Museum has the biggest mouse you've ever seen.**

A car-sized "mouse" controls the cursor on the Computer Museum's giant color monitor. The mouse floats on air—so you can move it.

UNSCRAMBLE THE WORDS

KDSI _____

OMEUS _____

AEDYRBOK _____

IORMNTO _____

Unscramble each word and match it to the computer part it describes.

BOSTON TEA PARTY SHIP AND MUSEUM

⬆ The *Beaver II*

Even if you don't drink tea, you probably know about the Boston Tea Party. It was the most famous tea party ever. One night in December 1773, some angry patriots (disguised as Mohawk Indians) crept aboard three British brigs at Griffin's Wharf. The ships were loaded with English tea. To protest Britain's taxes on tea and other goods, the patriots dumped 342 chests of tea into the harbor.

The *Beaver II* is a copy of one of the brigs. You can explore its decks, galley, quarters, and cargo hold. The modern-day crew will explain the ship's rigging. At the museum, you'll see films and exhibits.

Before leaving, you can throw your own bale of tea into the harbor. But times have changed. You have to pull it back up with a rope!

The tea that the patriots dumped into the harbor weighed 45 tons. That's 90,000 pounds!

HELP THE SAILOR

FINISH

START

The sailor is finished doing his work in the cargo hold. Can you help him find his way back up to the main deck?

MUSEUM OF SCIENCE

Yikes—science strikes! The exhibits at the Museum of Science are alive. On the **Live Animal Stage**, snakes and porcupines greet you. In the **Human Body Discovery Space**, you might ride a bike with a skeleton—and discover your own. In the **Thomson Theater of Electricity**, there's a live bolt of lightning.

Other exhibits invite you to be a scientist. You'll ask questions, collect data, and draw conclusions. You'll examine mystery objects and try to figure out what they are—or were.

The **Charles Hayden Planetarium** has laser shows and exhibits about the universe. On Friday nights, you can study stars from the rooftop observatory. Watching a show on the huge screen of the **Mugar Omni Theater**, you might forget you're even *in* a theater!

↑ **Electricity in action!**

The Mugar Omni Theater's domed screen is 5 stories high. It's the biggest screen in Boston.

← **Examine crystals up close.**

CONNECT THE DOTS

At the planetarium, you'll learn about the stars in the sky.
Connect the dots to find a famous constellation (group of stars).
What is the constellation's name?

M.I.T. MUSEUM

Warning: In case you think you don't like math, you might soon *change your mind!*

MIT stands for the Massachusetts Institute of Technology. Students here study math, science, and technology. Later, some of them invent things—like the things you're about to discover.

At **MathSpace**, you can create your own three-dimensional sculptures. At the MIT **Hall of Hacks**, you'll learn what a hack is, then see some things MIT hacks have made. Other exhibits let you use light and electricity to make special effects. Whatever you do, don't miss the holography exhibit! The MIT Museum has the biggest collection of holograms in the world. You will see examples from the 1940s through the present. The question is— can you believe your eyes?

⬆ *Tigirl* by Margaret Benyon is one of many holograms you can see.

The MIT Museum Shop has wild and wonderful books, games, puzzles, posters, and toys. It's almost as much fun as the museum!

FUN AT THE MUSEUM

Without telling what you're doing, ask someone for a word to fill in each blank. For example, say, "Give me an action word." When all the blanks are filled in, read the story out loud. One of the blanks has been filled in for you.

Dana took her friend Julee to the museum. "Let's go see the holograms first," said Dana.

"____Hey____!" Julee declared when they got to the exhibit. "I've
      exclamation

never seen so many holograms in one _____ before."
                                        object

The girls had a _____ time _____ing them from
                describing word   action word

different angles. "They look so real," said Dana, as she and Julee left

to see another exhibit.

"These sculptures look real too," said Julee. "Look at the

_____ cake." She reached out to touch it.
 flavor

"Hey!" _____ed a museum worker _____ing nearby.
        sound   action word

"That's no sculpture. It's my _____."
                               object

HARVARD MUSEUM OF CULTURAL AND NATURAL HISTORY

⇑ **The Mineralogical Museum is a gem!**

A glyptodont skull from Argentina

If you love Earth and its creatures, you won't want to miss this world-famous museum at Harvard University. It combines four museums in one building.

At the **Museum of Comparative Zoology**, you can examine what's left of a 42-foot plesiosaur or a 7-foot, 10-inch turtle. Meet Teleoceras, the "preposterous rhinoceros." Watch out for the glyptodont!

The **Peabody Museum**'s Hall of the American Indian focuses on cultures such as the Inuit, Navajo, and Maya.

The **Botanical Museum** has 847 life-size plant models, handmade from glass. From roots to petals, the flowers could fool a bee.

The **Mineralogical Museum** has glittering rocks and gems. Some crystals might even be taller than you.

WHAT'S THE DIFFERENCE?

**These two pictures of Indian villages might look the same, but they are not.
How many differences between the two drawings can you find?**

JOHN F. KENNEDY LIBRARY AND MUSEUM

The John F. Kennedy Library and Museum is a memorial to the 35th president of the United States, John Fitzgerald Kennedy (JFK), and his brother Robert Kennedy. President Kennedy was shot and killed in 1964. Robert Kennedy was shot and killed in 1968, when he was hoping to be elected president.

The Kennedys are one of Boston's most famous families. Throughout the 1900s, many Kennedy family members have worked in Massachusetts and national politics.

At the museum, you can see films about the Kennedys and watch parts of JFK's speeches. At the exhibits, you might find some surprises. Look at the president's report card. How did his grades compare to yours?

Take time to read "A Plea for a Raise," which the future president wrote when he was seven. Would *you* have raised his allowance?

⬆ **Young JFK (left) with his sisters and father**

On weekends, the Kennedy Library and Old Town Trolley Tours offer a 3-hour tour— "JFK's Boston." The trolley goes to places that were important in JFK's life.

YOU ARE THE PRESIDENT

**Imagine you are president of the United States.
Draw yourself in the Oval Office. Then color the scene.**

BOSTON MUSEUM OF FINE ARTS

The Boston Museum of Fine Arts is what you might call an important big-city museum. It has cool exhibits of all kinds—but not just for grown-ups. There are paintings, sculptures, drawings, and prints. There are objects made from gold, clay, glass, rock, wool, and wood. You can see art from around the world, from any time in history.

If you're here on a Tuesday, Wednesday, or Thursday afternoon (except in June), visit the Children's Room. It has art projects for kids. You can study art in the museum, then create your own. You might make a drawing, painting, poem, or kind of art that doesn't have a name yet. Or you might dance or make music.

On Sunday (October–June), the museum offers Family Place, with self-guided museum activities and activity booklets for parents and kids.

⇡ **The Rotunda at the MFA is awesome from top to bottom.**

Kids always get in for free at the MFA! Call ahead for a schedule.

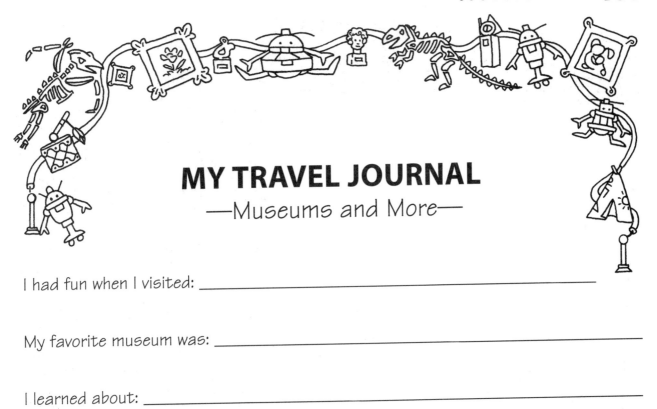

MY TRAVEL JOURNAL
—Museums and More—

I had fun when I visited: _____

My favorite museum was: _____

I learned about: _____

This is a picture of a painting or sculpture I saw

ON THE TOWN

WOULD YOU RATHER READ A BOOK
or hear a story? Go to a play or
to a concert? There are so many
ways to be entertained in
Boston, it's hard to decide.
Special events happen all year.
You could see Walt Disney's
World on Ice in February or
Barnum and Bailey Circus in
October. Check the *Boston
Globe*'s Thursday Calendar to
see what's going on.

⬆ **Puppets are the stars at Puppet Showplace Theatre.**

What if traveling makes you hungry?
This is Beantown, remember? You can get Boston baked beans, Indian
pudding, or Boston cream pie. Bostonians like New England clam
chowder (made with cream), lobster (whole), and scrod (codfish).
They like their oysters raw! And they love any food that's Italian. But if
you don't, don't worry. Boston has every kind of food in the world.

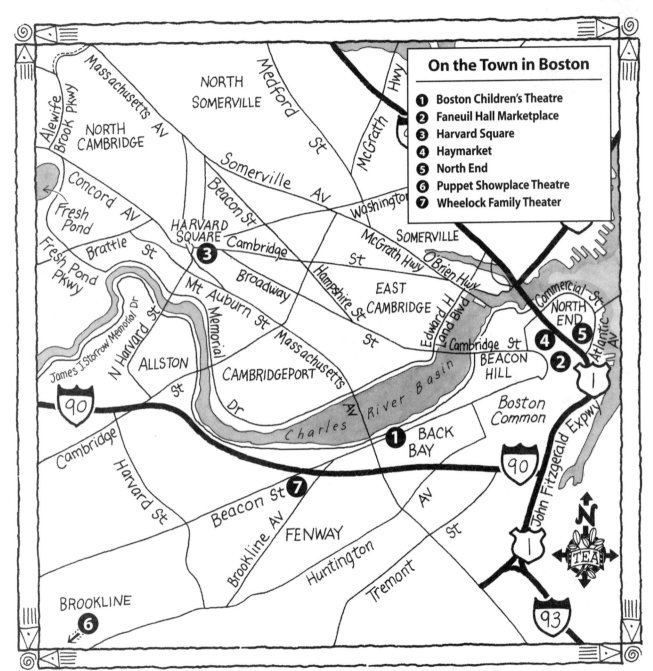

On the Town in Boston

1. Boston Children's Theatre
2. Faneuil Hall Marketplace
3. Harvard Square
4. Haymarket
5. North End
6. Puppet Showplace Theatre
7. Wheelock Family Theater

↥ **Fun at Faneuil Hall Marketplace**

Boston's small Chinatown is near Back Bay. There you'll find Asian markets and restaurants. Try a Vietnamese soup kitchen!

FANEUIL HALL MARKETPLACE

At Faneuil Hall Marketplace you can find a dolphin-shaped balloon, a T-shirt, or a souvenir from Boston. You might see street mimes or acrobats. It's a good place to learn some history—and to eat.

In the Quincy Market building (the one with the huge columns), you'll find fast food from around the world. You'll find English fish and chips, Greek moussaka, American pizza, Italian ices—you name it.

Or you can try an outdoor café or a restaurant. **Durgin Park**, in the North Market building, is the oldest, most famous restaurant here. It serves traditional Boston foods, at tables you share with strangers. The helpings are huge!

Across North Street, at 41 Union Street, is **Ye Olde Union Oyster House**, where people have been slurping raw oysters since 1826. If you aren't brave enough to try some, at least peek through the window.

HIDDEN MESSAGE

Cross out the B's, F's, H's, M's, P's, and W's.
Circle the remaining letters to find a secret
message sent by a Boston visitor.

F B W H P M I H B F P M F
H P H F B F H B F M H P B
W F L M O W V P E H B H M
P H P F M B P F W F H F P
B E M A F T H I P N W G W
H B F P H W B M F B H M P
O F Y W S B T H E W R P S

Write the hidden message here:

_____

_____

THE HAYMARKET

On Friday and Saturday, you will find the Haymarket on Blackstone Street—across North Street from Quincy Market. This is a noisy, crowded, wonderful place to get fresh fruits, vegetables, meats, and fish. Many vendors are Italian Americans who continue their family's tradition of selling food from pushcarts.

⇑ **You won't leave the Haymarket hungry.**

The fish stands are around the corner. The butcher shops are downstairs. Yes, those really are pigs' feet and lambs' heads—the way you would see them in a butcher shop in Italy.

There have been butcher shops here since 1666. In 1776 George Washington crossed a bridge over Mill Creek, which used to be right here. But the creek probably didn't smell good. The butchers tossed their garbage into the water!

Why is it called the Haymarket? In the old days, the carts were drawn by horses. The hay was for them.

WORD SEARCH

Hidden in this puzzle are the names of fruits and vegetables that you might find at an outdoor market. Search for words vertically, horizontally, and diagonally. Can you find all 12 words? The first word has been found for you.

Word Box

tomato	carrot	grapes
apple	potato	beans
banana	corn	onion
peach	squash	orange

```
T E N A T K M L S O P M Y P V U
H O H F R D P S P M H E B A O N
N N M L S G E P N O P T S B L T
T I P A P P L E A T T N G U L U
R O T W T M D A B B T A N T O D
S N U E M O H C A R R O T T R E
O Q S B G U N H N U I U R O A W
J T U E L W S H A K C L A R N D
P O U A U C O R N E S A N F G Q
U I S N S S G R A P E S G L E U
R O T S L H I T E U L I E Y N F
```

THE NORTH END

The North End is a great place to explore when you're hungry! It's one of Boston's oldest neighborhoods. First English Americans lived here, then Irish and Jewish, now Italian. You'll find small Italian restaurants and food shops along the main streets (Hanover and Salem) and some smaller ones.

As in Italy, most of the food shops here sell one main kind of food. It might be cheese (*formaggio*), bread (*pane*), meat (*carne*), ice cream (*gelato*), or pasta (*pasta*). There are bakeries with *biscotti*, sandwich shops with *calzone*, and places to sip hot *cioccolata*.

During July and August, the North End celebrates Catholic saints' festivals and feast days. There are religious parades in the streets, strings of streetlights, and, of course, more delicious food. *Buon appetito!*

⇑ The *Bocca di Verità* on Hanover Street tells your fortune.

In 1919 a tank broke in a North End factory. Two million gallons of hot molasses, 15 feet deep, drowned 21 people (and horses) in the street!

HIDE AND SEEK

**Can you find the hidden objects in this restaurant? When you
find one, circle it. Look for a bell, hand, butterfly, boot, penguin, pencil,
chicken leg, sucker, banana, ladybug, ice cream cone, baseball bat,
heart, and candle. When you're done, color the picture.**

PLAYS AND STORIES

Wheelock Family Theater performs plays and musicals by and for people of all different ages and from all over the world. Performances include sign language interpretation.

Boston Children's Theatre performs classic fairy tales and Broadway musicals—for kids and *by* kids. The Stagemobile is a traveling group of Boston Children's Theatre actors who perform in local parks during summer. In October the company offers *The Enchanted Forest*. In this play, the audience follows an outdoor trail and sees some magical things along the way.

Puppet Showplace Theatre has been entertaining kids and adults for 23 years. Every show is different. The stars might be hand-held puppets, marionettes, or shadow puppets. The theater is small, so call in advance for tickets.

⬆ **Boston Children's Theatre Stagemobile**

To hear a good story any time, call the Somerville Public Library's Dial-a-Story line (617-776-6531) or the Children's Discovery Museum Story Phone (508-264-4222).

WHICH ARE SIMILAR?

Each of these puppets has something in common with two others.
Draw a line connecting the puppets of the same type.

CAMBRIDGE

The heart of Cambridge is **Harvard Square** (which *isn't* square!). In warm weather fun things happen on the street. You might see a one-man band, a puppet show, or magic tricks. A tightrope walker might juggle burning torches! Folk singers might perform in Spanish or French.

↟ **You'll hear music in Harvard Square.**

For great games, software, videos, toys, and telescopes, visit **Learningsmith**. A block away, **Cybersmith** is a computer play space where you can pay a dollar to explore the computers and their software all day. **Curious George Goes to WordsWorth** is a bookstore where kids get their words' worth, at a discount.

If you get hungry at Harvard Square, there are plenty of inexpensive restaurants. At **Au Bon Pain**, near the Ⓣ stop, you can eat outside while watching a chess game.

↟ **You might also hear a story.**

MY TRAVEL JOURNAL
—On the Town—

These are the names of the places I visited: _____

My favorite place was: _____

The strangest thing I saw was: _____

This is a picture of something I saw

CALENDAR OF EVENTS

January

Martin Luther King Jr. Day
Events throughout the area, at schools, libraries, museums, and theaters.

February

Black History Month
Boston, (617) 742-5415. Cambridge, (617) 349-4040. Events throughout the area at schools, libraries, museums, and theaters.

Chinese New Year
Chinatown, Boston, (617) 426-8858. Lion dances and firecrackers chase away evil spirits. Special treats bring good luck.

March

Maple Sugaring Season
Massachusetts Audubon Sanctuaries, (617) 259-9500. Maple Producers Association, (413) 628-3912. Maple syrup making.

St. Patrick's Day
South Boston, (617) 536-4100 or 268-8525. Parade with floats and bagpipe bands.

April

Street Performers' Festival
Faneuil Hall Marketplace, Boston, (617) 446-8364. Music, food, entertainers.

Lantern Service
Old North Church, Boston, (617) 523-6676. Reenactment of the hanging of lanterns in the steeple.

Patriot's Day
Lexington, (617) 862-1450. Concord, (617) 369-6944. Revolutionary War reenactments begin at dawn on Patriot's Day (third Monday in April). Pancake breakfasts and parades follow.

Boston Marathon
Boston, (508) 435-6905 or (617) 236-1652. Patriot's Day race from Hopkinton to Copley Square.

May

Kite Festival

Franklin Park, Boston, (617) 635-4505. Kite making and flying, contests, music, acrobatics, and food.

Ducklings Day Parade

Beacon Hill to the Public Garden, Boston, (617) 426-1885. On Mother's Day, children join the parade, dressed as their favorite characters from Robert McCloskey's *Make Way for Ducklings*.

June

Boston Dairy Festival

Boston Common, (617) 734-6750. Farm animals, petting zoo, cow milking, and food.

Bunker Hill Day

Bunker Hill and Charlestown Navy Yard, Charlestown, (617) 242-5628 or 242-5601. Eighteenth-century military encampment, parades.

St. Botolph's Street Fair

Boston, (617) 536-3310. Face painting, clowns, balloons, food, and entertainment.

St. Peter's Fiesta

St. Peter's Square, Gloucester, (508) 283-1601. Fireworks, music, sporting events, parade, blessing of the fishing fleet.

Salem Maritime Festival

Salem, (508) 745-1470. Boatbuilding, sail making, and quilting demonstrations. Tall ships, music, and food.

July

Harborfest Esplanade Celebration

Boston, (617) 227-1528. Celebration of Boston's maritime history. Fireworks, concerts, food, boat rides, and historic reenactments.

Boston Pops Fourth of July Concert

Charles River Esplanade, Boston, (617) 266-1492. Fireworks over the Charles River accompany the orchestra's grand finale.

Chowderfest

City Hall Plaza, Boston, (617) 227-1528. Celebration featuring the famous Boston food.

Italian Feast Days

North End, Boston, (617) 536-4100 or (800) 888-5515. Street festivals honoring Roman Catholic saints. Italian food and Sicilian music.

August

August Moon Festival

Chinatown, Boston, (617) 426-8858. Festival celebrating Chinese Thanksgiving–when the moon is full. Parades, music, dance, and moon cakes for good luck.

Teddy Bear Rally
Town Common, Amherst, (413) 256-8983. Teddy bear celebration. Entertainment, teddy bear hospital.

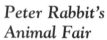

Peter Rabbit's Animal Fair
Sandwich, (508) 888-6870. Appearances by Peter Rabbit and Smokey the Bear. Animals, music, storytelling, and food.

Italian Feast Days
North End, Boston, (617) 536-4100 or (800) 888-5515. Street festivals honoring Roman Catholic saints. Italian food and Sicilian music.

September

Cambridge River Festival
Memorial Drive, Cambridge, (617) 349-4380. Arts, food, and entertainment.

October

Cranberry Harvest Festival
Cranberry World, off Route 58, South Carver, (508) 747-2350. Celebration features a harvest of red berries floating in bogs.

Head of the Charles Regatta
Charles River, Cambridge, (617) 864-8415 or 466-6208. World's largest single-day rowing race.

Haunted Happenings
Salem, (508) 744-0004. Halloween celebration featuring treasure hunts, candlelight tours of historic homes, haunted houses, Eerie Events, Psychic Fair.

Harvest Moon Festival
Charles Square (off Harvard Square), Cambridge, (617)864-1200. Food, farm produce, musicians, storytellers, and exhibit of children's art.

Kidsfest
Wachusett Mountain, Princeton, (508) 464-2300. Arts and crafts, food, sky-rides to the summit.

November

Thanksgiving Celebrations
Plymouth, (508) 746-3377. Plimoth Plantation, (508) 746-1622. Old Sturbridge Village, (800) SEE-1830 or (508) 347-3362.

December

Boston Common Tree Lighting
Boston Common, (617) 635-4505.
Tree lighting and carol singing.

Boston Tea Party Reenactment
Boston, (617) 338-1773. On December 16
costumed "Sons of Liberty" head from the
Old South Meeting House to the Boston Tea Party
Ship, where they throw chests of tea overboard.

Kwanzaa
Children's Museum, (617) 426-6500. Art of Black
Dance and Music, (617) 666-1859. Traditional
African harvest celebrations between December 26
and January 1.

First Night
Boston, (617) 542-1399. New Year's Eve
celebration featuring parade, ice sculptures,
countdown to midnight, and fireworks over Boston
Harbor.

For more information and more events, check:
The Boston Globe Calendar, Thursday edition
The Boston Phoenix, Friday edition

RESOURCE GUIDE: WHEN, WHAT, AND WHERE?

The information in this Resource Guide changes often. For current days and times, call before you go.

If You Get Lost

Do you know what to do if you get lost? Make a plan with your parents about what to do if you lose them. If you forget what to do and you're in a store, go to a person working at a cash register. If you are outside, look for a mother with children. Tell her you're lost.

If there is an emergency and you need the police, fire department, or an ambulance, dial 911 from any phone. You won't need coins.

Important Numbers

Injury, accident, or emergency: 911
If you get separated from your family: 911
Boston Police: (617) 343-4200
Cambridge Police: (617) 349-3300
Poison Control Center: (617) 232-2120
Travelers Aid Society of Boston: (617) 542-7286

Transportation

Ferries:
Bay State Cruise Company, (617) 723-7800
Steamship Authority, (508) 477-8600

Water Shuttle:
Boston By Boat, (617) 422-0392 or (800) 235-6426

Trolley Tours:
Beantown Trolley, (617) 236-2148
Blue Trolley Tours, (617) 269-3626
Boston Duck Tours, (617) 723-DUCK
Old Town Trolley Tours, (617) 269-7150

Subway, Buses, and Commuter Rail:
MBTA, (617) 722-3200 or (800) 392-6100

Where They Are and When They're Open

Abiel Smith School, 46 Joy Street. Open daily, 10 a.m.–4 p.m. (617) 742-5415.

African Meeting House, 8 Smith Court, Boston. Open daily, 10 a.m.–4 p.m. (617) 742-5415.

Arnold Arboretum, 125 Arborway, Jamaica Plain. Open daily. (617) 524-1718.

Battle Road Visitor Center, Minute Man National Historical Park, Route 2A, Lexington. Open mid-April through October. (617) 862-7753.

Big Apple Circus, Boston.
Open end of March
through early
May. Call for location,
(617) 426-6500, ext. 666.

**Black Heritage Trail,
Boston.** Ranger-led tours
in summer. (617) 742-
5415.

BosTix Ticket Booths, Faneuil Hall Marketplace
and Copley Square, Boston. Tickets for some
performances. Open Tuesday through Saturday,
10 a.m.–6 p.m., Sunday, 11 a.m.–4 p.m.
(617) 482-BTIX.

Boston African American National Historic Site,
46 Joy Street, Boston. Open daily, 10 a.m.–4 p.m.
(617) 742-5415.

Boston Bruins, FleetCenter, Causeway Street,
Boston. Call for schedule, (617) 624-1000.

Boston By Boat. Water shuttle to neighborhoods
and attractions. Open daily, late May to September.
Open weekends, September to mid-October. Call for
times. (617) 422-0392 or (800) 235-6426.

Boston By Foot. Neighborhood walking tours,
including Boston for Little Feet (children's tours of
the Freedom Trail). Call for information,
(617) 367-2345.

Boston Celtics, FleetCenter, Causeway Street,
Boston. Call for schedule. (617) 523-3030.

Boston Children's Theatre, 4th
floor, 647 Boylston (Copley Square),
Boston. Call for schedule and
tickets. (617) 424-6634.

Boston Common, between Park,
Charles, Tremont, and Beacon Streets, Boston.
Frog Pond Pavilion, wading pond and ice-skating
rink, open seasonally. Call Department of Parks and
Recreation for information, (617) 635-7383.

Boston Common Visitor Information Center, 147
Tremont Street (near the Park Street Ⓣ station),
Boston. Open Monday through Saturday, 8:30
a.m.–5 p.m., Sunday, 9 a.m.–5 p.m. (617)
536-4100 or (800) 888-1515.

Boston Harbor Islands. Ranger-led tours. July
through August, open daily, 10 a.m.–3 p.m. Call for
departure points. (617) 740-1605.

Boston Marathon, Patriot's Day race from
Hopkinton to Copley Square, Boston. Call for time
and route, (617) 236-1652 or (508) 435-6905.

Boston Massacre Site, next to Old State House
(on traffic island), Boston.

Boston National Historical Park Visitor Center,
15 State Street, Boston. Open daily, 9 a.m.–5 p.m.,
in summer until 6 p.m. Call for information on
Freedom Trail and other tours, (617) 242-5642.

Boston Parks and Recreation Department, Boston Common Visitor Center, Park and Tremont Streets, Boston. Call for information, (617) 635-7383.

Boston Red Sox, Fenway Park, Yawkey Way, Boston. Call for schedule and tickets, (617) 267-1700.

Boston Tea Party Ship and Museum, Congress Street Bridge, Boston. Call for hours, (617) 338-1773.

Bunker Hill Monument, Monument Square, Charlestown. Open daily. (617) 242-5641.

Bunker Hill Pavilion, 55 Constitution Road, Charlestown. Open daily, 9 a.m.–5 p.m., June through August until 6 p.m. (617) 241-7575.

Cambridge Office for Tourism. Call Monday through Friday, 9 a.m.–5 p.m. (617) 441-2884 or (800) 862-5678.

Cambridge Visitor Information Booth, Harvard Square (by the Ⓣ station), Cambridge. Open Monday through Saturday, 9 a.m.–5 p.m., Sunday, 1–5 p.m.

Cape Cod National Seashore, South Wellfleet. (508) 349-3785.

Cape Cod Rail Trail, connecting Dennis, Brewster, Eastham, and Wellfleet. (617) 727-3180 or (800) 831-0569 (in Massachusetts).

Children's Museum, 300 Congress Street, Boston. Open Tuesday through Sunday, 10 a.m.–5 p.m., Friday, 10 a.m.–9 p.m. (617) 426-8855.

Community Boating, 21 Embankment Road, Boston, Call for hours and information, (617) 523-1038.

Computer Museum, 300 Congress Street, Boston. Open Tuesday through Sunday, 10 a.m.–5 p.m. (617) 426-2800.

Concord Museum, 200 Lexington Road, Concord. Call for hours, (508) 369-9609.

⬆ **Community Boating**

Concord Visitor Center, Heywood Street (1 block from Concord Center), Concord. Open seasonally. (508) 369-3120.

Copp's Hill Burial Ground, Hull Street, uphill from Old North Church, Boston. Open 9 a.m. to dusk.

Cranberry World Visitors Center, 225 Water Street, Plymouth. May through November, open daily, 9:30 a.m.–5 p.m. (508) 747-2350.

Curious George Goes to WordsWorth, 1 JFK Street, Cambridge. Open Monday through Saturday, 9 a.m.–11:15 p.m., Sunday, 10 a.m.–10:15 p.m. (617) 498-0062.

Cybersmith, 42 Church Street, Cambridge; South canopy of Quincy Market building in Faneuil Hall Marketplace, Boston. Call for hours: Cambridge, (617) 492-5857, Boston, (617) 367-1777.

Drumlin Farm Wildlife Sanctuary, Route 117, South Great Road, Lincoln. Open Tuesday through Sunday and Monday holidays, 9 a.m.–4 p.m. (617) 259-9807.

Durgin Park Restaurant, North Market Building, Faneuil Hall Marketplace, Boston. Open daily, 11:30 a.m.–10 p.m. (617) 227-2038.

Faneuil Hall Marketplace, Merchants Row, off Congress Street between North and State Streets, Boston.

Faneuil Hall, Merchants Row, off Congress Street, Boston. Open daily, 9 a.m.–5 p.m. Closed for special functions. (617) 242-5642.

Fenway Park, Gate D, Yawkey Way and Van Ness Street, Boston. Tours beginning in May, Monday through Friday, 10 a.m., 11 a.m., 12 p.m., and 1 p.m. (617) 236-6666.

Franklin Park Zoo, 1 Franklin Park Road, Boston. Open daily, 10 a.m.–4 p.m. Call for directions, (617) 442-2002.

Freedom Trail. Ranger-led walking tours. For information contact Boston National Historical Park Visitor Center, 15 State Street, Boston. Open daily, 9 a.m.–5 p.m., in summer until 6 p.m. (617) 242-5642.

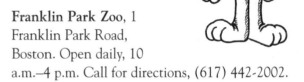

Granary Burying Ground, Tremont Street, next to Park Street Church, Boston. Open 9 a.m. to dusk.

Greater Boston Convention and Visitors Bureau, Visitor Kiosk, Center Court, Prudential Center, Boston. Open Monday through Friday, 8:30 a.m.–6 p.m., Saturday, 10 a.m.–6 p.m., Sunday, 11:30 a.m.–6 p.m. (617) 536-4100 or (888) SEE-BOSTON.

Green Briar Nature Center, 6 Discovery Hill Road, East Sandwich. Open Tuesday through Saturday in winter, daily spring through fall, 10 a.m.–4 p.m. (508) 888-6870.

Harvard Museum of Cultural and Natural History, 24 Oxford Street and 11 Divinity Avenue, Cambridge. Open Monday through Saturday, 9 a.m.–5 p.m., Sunday, 1–5 p.m. (617) 495-1910 or (617) 495-2248.

House of the Seven Gables, 54 Turner Street, Salem. Open daily. Call for hours, (508) 744-0991.

John F. Kennedy Library and Museum, Columbia Point, Boston. Open daily, 9 a.m.–5 p.m. (617) 929-4523.

John Hancock Observatory, 200 Clarendon Street, Boston. Open Monday through Saturday, 9 a.m.–10 p.m., Sunday, noon to 10 p.m. (617) 572-6429.

King's Chapel, corner of School and Tremont Streets, Boston. Open daily. Call for hours, (617) 227-2155.

Learningsmith, 25 Brattle Street, Cambridge. Open daily, 10 a.m.–10 p.m. (617) 661-6008.

Lexington Visitor Center, 1875 Massachusetts Avenue, Lexington. Open daily. (617) 862-1450.

⬆ **Quincy Market**

Lowell National Historical Park, Visitor Center, 246 Market Street, Lowell. Exhibits and tours by foot, trolley, and canal barge. Open daily. Call for hours, (508) 970-5000.

Make Way for Ducklings, Historic Neighborhoods Foundation, 99 Bedford Street, Boston. Kids' walking tour based on Robert McCloskey's story. Also ask about A Kid's View: walking tours of the North End, Chinatown, and the Waterfront. Late spring through fall. Call for information and reservations, (617) 426-1885.

Massachusetts Office of Travel and Tourism, 100 Cambridge Street, 13th floor, Boston. Open Monday through Friday, 9 a.m.–5 p.m. (617) 727-3201.

Massachusetts State Forests and Parks,
100 Cambridge Street, Boston. Guided walks and educational programs from mid-June to September. (617) 727-3180.

Minute Man National Historical Park, Route 2A, Lexington; 174 Liberty Street, Concord. April through October, open daily, 8:30 a.m.–5 p.m. (617) 862-7753 in Lexington, (508) 369-6993 in Concord.

Minuteman Bikeway, connecting Cambridge, Arlington, Lexington, and Bedford. (617) 641-4891.

MIT Museum,
265 Massachusetts Avenue, Cambridge. Open Tuesday through Friday, 10:00 a.m.–5:00 p.m., Saturday and Sunday 12–5 p.m. (617) 253-4444.

Museum of Fine Arts, 465 Huntington Avenue, Boston. Open daily. Call for hours and schedule of kids' activities. (617) 267-9300.

Museum of Our National Heritage, Route 2A and Massachusetts Avenue, Lexington. Open Monday through Saturday, 10 a.m.–5 p.m., Sunday, 12–5 p.m. (617) 861-6559.

Museum of Science, Science Park, Boston. Open daily, 9 a.m.–5 p.m., Fridays until 9 p.m. Call for reservations. (617) 723-2500 or 227-3235.

New Bedford Whaling Museum, 18 Johnny Cake Hill, New Bedford. Open daily, 9 a.m.–5 p.m. (508) 997-0046.

New England Aquarium, Central Wharf, Boston. Call for hours, (617) 973-5200.

New England Holocaust Memorial, between Union and Congress Streets, Boston.

New England Patriots. Call for football schedule, location, and tickets, (508) 543-1776.

⬆ **The IMAX Theater at the Museum of Science**

Nickerson State Park, Route 6A, Brewster (on Cape Cod). Open daily, dawn to dusk. (508) 896-3491.

North Bridge Visitor Center, Minute Man National Historical Park, 174 Liberty Street, Concord. Park and visitor center open daily. Call for hours, (508) 369-6993 or (617) 484-6156.

Old Corner Bookstore, 1 School Street, Boston. Open Monday through Friday, 9 a.m.–6:30 p.m., Saturday, 9 a.m.–6 p.m., Sunday, 12–6 p.m. (617) 523-6658.

Old North Bridge, Monument Street, Concord.

Old North Church, 193 Salem Street, Boston. Open daily, 9 a.m.–5 p.m. Services: Sunday, 9 a.m., 11 a.m., and 4 p.m. (617) 523-6676.

Old South Meeting House, 310 Washington Street, Boston. Scheduled to reopen in fall 1997. Call for hours. (617) 482-6439.

Old State House, 206 Washington Street, Boston. Open daily, 9:30 a.m.–5 p.m. (617) 720-3290.

Old Sturbridge Village, 1 Old Sturbridge Village Road, Sturbridge. Call for hours and events, (508) 347-3362 or (800) SEE-1830.

Orchard House, 399 Lexington Road, Concord. Open daily, mid-January through December. Call for hours, (508) 369-4118.

Park Street Church, 1 Park Street, Boston. Open July and August only, Tuesday through Saturday, 9 a.m.–3 p.m. (617) 523-3383.

Paul Revere House, 19 North Square, Boston. Open November through April 14, 9:30 a.m.–4:15

↑ **Massachusetts State House**

p.m., April 15 through October, 9:30 a.m.–5:15 p.m. Closed Monday, January through March. (617) 523-2338.

Peabody Essex Museum, East India Square, Salem. Open Tuesday through Saturday, 10 a.m.–5 p.m. (Friday till 8 p.m.), Sunday, 12–5 p.m. (508) 745-1876.

Plimoth Plantation, 133 Warren Avenue, Route 3A, Plymouth. *Mayflower II*, State Pier, Plymouth. Open daily, April through November. Call for hours and special events. (508) 746-1622.

Plymouth Rock, Water Street, Plymouth.

Public Garden, between Arlington and Charles Streets, Boston. Open daily. Swan Boats, available mid-April through September. (617) 522-1966.

Puppet Showplace Theatre, 32 Station Street, Brookline Village. Performances: September through June, Saturdays and Sundays, 1 p.m. and 3 p.m., July and August, Thursdays, 10:30 a.m. and 1 p.m. (617) 731-6400.

Rebecca Nurse Homestead, Danvers. Open in summer. Call for hours, (508)774-8799.

Quincy Market (see Faneuil Hall Marketplace).

Salem Witch Museum, 19 ¹/₂ Washington Square North, Salem. Open daily, 10 a.m.–5 p.m., July

and August, 10 a.m.–7 p.m. (800) 544-1692 or (508) 744-1692.

Site of the First Public School and Franklin Statue, School Street, Boston.

State House, Beacon Hill, Boston. Monday through Friday, 10 a.m.–4 p.m. Tours every half hour. (617) 727-3676.

Stone Zoo, Stoneham. Open daily, 10 a.m.–4 p.m. Call for directions, (617) 442-2002.

Trinity Church, Copley Square, Boston. Open daily. (617) 536-0944.

USS *Cassin Young*, Pier 1, Charlestown Navy Yard, Charlestown. Open daily, 10 a.m.–4 p.m. Tour times vary. (617) 242-5601.

USS *Constitution*, Pier 1, Charlestown Navy Yard, Charlestown. Open daily, 9:30 a.m. to sunset. Tours until 3:50 p.m. (617) 242-5670 or 242-5671.

USS Constitution Museum, Charlestown Navy Yard, Charlestown. Open daily. Call for hours. (617) 426-1812.

Wachusett Mountain, Mountain Road, Princeton. Downhill ski area. Call for hours. (800) SKI-1234.

Walden Pond State Reservation, Walden Street (Route 126), Concord. Open sunrise to sunset, but closed earlier if crowds become too great. From June to September, call ahead. (508) 369-3254.

Whale Watching, New England Aquarium, Central Wharf, Boston. April through October. Call for schedule and information, (617) 973-5277.

Wheelock Family Theatre, 180 The Riverway, Boston. Box office open Monday through Friday, 12–5:30 p.m. (617) 734-4760. Tickets also available through BosTix, (617) 482-BTIX.

Witch Dungeon Museum, 16 Lynde Street, Salem. Call for hours. (508) 744-9812.

Ye Olde Union Oyster House, 41 Union Street, Boston (across from Faneuil Hall Marketplace). Open Sunday through Thursday, 11 a.m.–9:30 p.m., Friday and Saturday, 11 a.m.–10 p.m. (617) 227-2750.

ANSWERS TO PUZZLES

page
17

```
C H U R C H M E S O P M Y P V
H O H F R D Q S Y M W I T C H
N Y U L S G B O S T O N S B I
T T P N D R S M A T I D G U S
R A T W T M I R D V C I N F T
D E U E M R F N G T E A G R O
E D S R G U Y N H U I N Y E R
S A X L P C I N D K C S M E Y
P F I S H I N G W B O A T D L
U P S E I S U R N P Y D N O L
R O T B L K I T E U L I M M N
```

page
29

page
19

page
31

ACROSS	DOWN
2. bells	1. steeple
4. church	3. Massachusetts
5. pews	7. coal
6. England	
8. Puritan	

page
33

hundred
dollar
bill

page
39

Here are some of the words you can make using the letters in the word FANEUIL:

ail	flea	lean
an	fuel	lie
fail	fun	life
fan	if	line
file	in	nail
fin	lane	
fine	leaf	

page
35

war pain**T**
tax **E** s
A merican
P atriot
h **A** rbor
B **R** itish
revolu **T** ion
libert **Y**

page
51

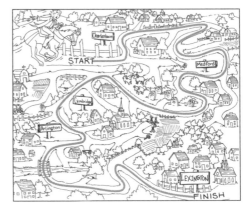

page
37

Redcoat

page
53

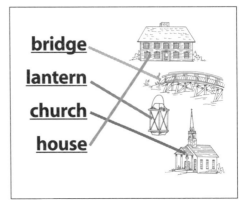

bridge

lantern

church

house

page 55

page 57

page 65

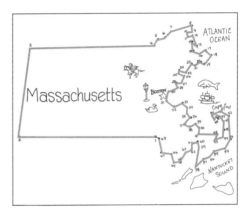

page 67

page 69

page 77

ACROSS
1. popcorn
3. bat
4. home run
5. rain

DOWN
2. pitcher
3. ball
6. Green
7. outs

130 ~~~~~~~~~~

page
79

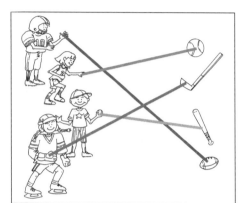

page
91

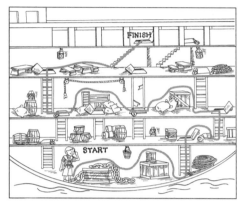

page
81

page
89

DISK

MOUSE

KEYBOARD

MONITOR

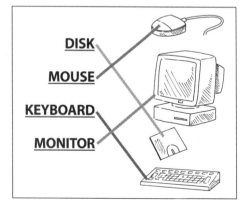

page
93

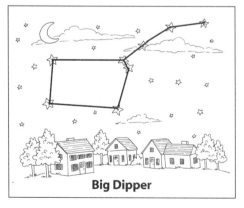

Big Dipper

page 97

page 105

I

LOVE

EATING

OYSTERS

page 109

page 107

```
T E N A T K M L S O P M Y P V U
H O H F R D P S P M H E B A O N
N N M L S G E P N O P T S B L T
T I I P A P P L E A T T N G U L U
R O T W T M D A B B T A N T O D
S N U E M O H C A R R O T T R E
O Q S B G U N H N U I U R O A W
J T U E L W S H A K C L A R N D
P O U A U C O R N E S A N F G Q
U I S N S S G R A P E S G L E U
R O T S L H I T E U L I E Y N F
```

page 111

GEOGRAPHICAL INDEX: WHERE IS EVERYTHING?

Back Bay
BosTix
Boston Children's Theatre
Copley Square
Greater Boston Convention and
    Visitors Bureau
John Hancock Observatory
Public Garden

Beacon Hill
Black Heritage Trail
Boston African American National
    Historic Site
Louisburg Square
State House

Brookline
Puppet Showplace Theatre

Cambridge
Cambridge Visitor Information Booth
Curious George Goes to WordsWorth
CyberSmith
Harvard Square
Harvard University Museums
Learningsmith
M.I.T. Museum

Charlestown
Bunker Hill Monument
Bunker Hill Pavilion
Charlestown Navy Yard
Freedom Trail sites
USS *Cassin Young*
USS *Constitution*
USS Constitution Museum

Chinatown
Asian food markets and restaurants
Chinatown gate

Dorchester
John F. Kennedy Library and Museum

Downtown
Boston Common
Boston National Historical Park
    Service Visitors Center
Community Boating
Durgin Park Restaurant
Faneuil Hall Marketplace
FleetCenter
Freedom Trail sites
The Haymarket
Museum of Science
New England Holocaust Memorial
Ye Olde Union Oyster House

East Boston
Logan Airport

The Fenway
Arnold Arboretum
Fenway Park
Museum of Fine Arts
Wheelock Family Theatre

The North End
Freedom Trail sites
Italian markets

Roxbury
Franklin Park Zoo

South End
Boston Tea Party Ship and Museum
Children's Museum
Computer Museum

Waterfront
New England Aquarium
Waterfront Park

Out of Town
Battle Road Visitors Center
Cape Cod National Seashore
Cape Cod Rail Trail
Concord Museum
Cranberry World
Green Briar Nature Center
Hancock-Clarke House
House of the Seven Gables
Lexington Battle Green
Lexington Visitor Center
Lowell National Historic Park
Martha's Vineyard
Minuteman Bikeway
Minute Man National Historical Park
Museum of Our National Heritage
Nantucket Island
New Bedford Whaling Museum
Nickerson State Park
Old North Bridge
Old Sturbridge Village
Orchard House
Peabody Museum (Salem)
Plimoth Plantation
Plymouth Rock
Rebecca Nurse Homestead
Salem Witch Museum
Stone Zoo
Wachusett Mountain
Walden Pond State Reservation

INDEX

A
Abiel Smith School, 20
Adams, Charles, 80
Adams, Samuel, 24, 28, 32, 50
African Americans, 10, 20, 36. *See also* Black Heritage Trail
African Meeting House, 20
African Tropical Forest, 68
Alcott, Louisa May, 18, 52
American Revolution. *See* Revolutionary War
Arnold Arboretum, 62
Attucks, Crispus, 36
Au Bon Pain, 112

B
Back Bay, 8, 104
Battle Road Visitor Center, 50
Beacon Hill, 8, 18, 20
Beaver II, 90
Best Software for Kids Gallery, 88
Bird, Larry, 78
Black Heritage Trail, 14, 20, 21
Blackstone, William, 18, 22
Boston Bruins, 74, 80
Boston Celtics, 74, 78
Boston Children's Theater, 110
Boston Common, 10, 16, 22, 62, 82
Boston for Little Feet, 13
Boston Harbor Islands, 64
Boston Latin School, 10, 32
Boston Light, 64
Boston Marathon, 74
Boston Massacre Site, 36
Boston Museum of Fine Arts, 100
Boston Red Sox, 74, 76
Boston Tea Party, 6, 34, 90
Botanical Museum, 96
Brimstone Corner, 26

Buckman Tavern, 50
Bulfinch, Charles, 24
Bull Gang, 78
Bunker Hill, Battle of, 7, 42, 46
Bunker Hill Monument, 46
Bunker Hill Pavilion, 46

C
Cambridge, Massachusetts, 82, 112
Cape Cod, 48, 64, 66
Cape Cod National Seashore, 66
Cape Cod Rail Trail, 66
Car-Free in Boston, 13
Charles Hayden Planetarium, 92
Charles River, 13, 62, 74, 82
Charlestown Bridge, 44
Charlestown, Massachusetts, 40
Charlestown Navy Yard, 44, 46
Children's Museum, 86
Chinatown, 14, 104
City Carpet, 32
Civil War, 10, 20
Community Boating, 62
Computer Museum, 88
Concord, Massachusetts, 7, 48, 52
Concord Museum, 52
Concord Visitor Center, 52
Copley Square, 16
Copp's Hill Burying Ground, 42
Cranberry World, 56
Curious George Goes to WordsWorth, 112
Custom House tower, 16
Cybersmith, 112

D
Dawes, William, 7
Declaration of Independence, 7, 28, 36

Dial-a-Story, 110
Discovery Pavilion, 72
Durgin Park, 104
Dyer, Mary, 24

E
England, 2, 4, 6, 36
Emerald Necklace, 62, 68, 82
Emerson, Ralph Waldo, 52
Esplanade, 62

F
Faneuil Hall, 38
Faneuil Hall Marketplace, 104
Faneuil, Peter, 38
Fenway Park, 14, 76
FleetCenter, 74, 78, 80
Founders' Monument, 22
Franklin, Benjamin, 28, 32
Franklin Park, 62
Franklin Park Zoo, 68
Franklin Statue, 32
Freedom Trail, 14, 22, 23, 38, 44
Frog Pond, 22

G
Garrison, William Lloyd, 26
Giant Ocean Tank, 72
Gloucester, Massachusetts, 4
Granary Burying Ground, 28
Great Elm tree, 22, 24
Greater Boston Convention & Visitors Bureau, 16
Green Briar Nature Center, 66
Green Monster, 76

H
Hall of Flags, 24
Hall of Hacks, 94

Hancock-Clarke House, 50
Hancock, John, 28, 32, 50
Harvard Museum of Cultural and Natural History, 96
Harvard Square, 112
Harvard University, 10
Hawthorne, Nathaniel, 34, 48, 52, 54
Haymarket, 106
Head of the Charles Regatta, 74
Hobbamock's Homesite, 56
House of the Seven Gables, 54
Human Body Discovery Space, 92
Hutchinson, Anne, 24

J
Jamaica Pond, 62
John F. Kennedy Library and Museum, 98
John Hancock Building, 14, 16

K
Kennedy, John F., 98
King's Chapel, 30

L
Learningsmith, 112
Lewis Hayden House, 20
Lexington Battle Green, 50
Lexington, Massachusetts, 7, 40, 48, 50
Lexington Visitor Center, 50
Little Brewster Island, 64
Live Animal Stage, 92
Longfellow, Henry Wadsworth, 7, 34
Lowell, Massachusetts, 48

M
Make Way for Ducklings (book), 62
Make Way for Ducklings (walking tour), 13
Martha's Vineyard, 64
Massachusetts, 2, 24, 36
Mathspace, 94
Mayflower, 5, 56
Mayflower II, 56
"Midnight Ride of Paul Revere," 7
Mineralogical Museum, 96
Minuteman Bikeway, 82
Minute Man National Historic Park, 50, 52

M.I.T. Museum, 94
Monroe Tavern, 50
Mother Goose, 28, 29
Mugar Omni Theater, 92
Museum of Comparative Zoology, 96
Museum of Our National Heritage, 50
Museum of Science, 84, 92
"My Country 'Tis of Thee," 26

N
Nantucket, 64
National Marine Fisheries Service Aquarium, 66
New England Aquarium, 70, 72
New England Holocaust Memorial, 38
Newman, Robert, 42, 52
Nickerson State Park, 66
North Bridge Visitor Center, 52
North End, 38, 108

O
Old Corner Bookstore, 34
"Old Ironsides," 44
Old North Bridge, 52
Old North Church, 7, 14, 42
Old South Meeting House, 34
Old State House, 36
Old Sturbridge Village, 58

P
Paine, Robert Treat, 28
Park Street Church, 26
Patriot's Day, 40, 50
Paul Revere House, 40
Paul Revere Mall, 40, 42
Peabody Museum (Harvard), 96
Peabody Museum (Salem), 54
Pilgrims, 4, 22, 48, 56
Pilgrim Village, 56
Plimoth Plantation, 45, 56
Plymouth, Massachusetts, 4, 48, 56
Plymouth Rock, 48, 56
Public Garden, 62, 82
Puppet Showplace Theatre, 102, 110
Puritans, 4, 22, 24, 34

Q
Quakers, 4, 22, 24
Quincy Market, 38, 104

R
Rebecca Nurse Homestead, 54
Revere, Paul, 7, 24, 28, 30, 40, 42, 50
Revolutionary War, 6, 7, 14, 34, 46, 48
Rivers of the Americas Gallery, 72
Robert Gould Shaw and 54th Regiment Memorial, 20

S
Sacred Cod, 24
Salem Maritime National Historic Site, 54
Salem, Massachusetts, 4, 48, 54
Salem Witch Museum, 54
Sons of Liberty, 6, 7, 40
State House, 14, 16, 24, 25
Stone Zoo, 68
Stowe, Harriet Beecher, 34
Sturbridge, Massachusetts, 48, 58
Swan Boats, 62

T
Thinking Gallery, 72
Thomson Theater of Electricity, 92
Thoreau, Henry David, 52
Trinity Church, 14

U
Underground Railroad, 20
U.S. Pro Tennis Championships, 74
USS *Cassin Young*, 44
USS *Constitution*, 15, 44
USS Constitution Museum, 44

W
Wachusett Mountain, 82
Walden Pond, 52
Walton, Bill, 78
Wampanoag Indians, 56
War of 1812, 26, 44
Waterfront Park, 62
Washington, George, 7, 42, 106
whale watching, 70
Wheelock Family Theater, 110
Witch Dungeon Museum, 54
witch trials, 4, 22, 48, 54

Y
Ye Olde Union Oyster House, 104

Photo Credits

Pages iii (top), 1, 2, 11 (bottom), 14, 15, 16 (bottom), 18, 36, 46, 56, 64, 66, 70, 76 (bottom), 82, 104, 120, 122, 124—© Kindra Clineff/Massachusetts Office of Travel and Tourism; Pages 16 (top), 62, 74—Greater Boston Convention and Visitors Bureau; Pages i, ii, iii (bottom), 10, 11, 12, 13, 20, 22, 24, 26, 30, 34, 60, 106, 108—©Helen Byers; Pages 4, 6, 7, 8—Courtesy of The Bostonian Society/Old State House; Pages 28, 32—Klein Postcard Service, Boston; Pages 38, 40, 42—National Park Service; Page 42—U.S. Navy; Page 48—Ted Curtin/Plimoth Plantation; Pages 50, 52—Minuteman National Historic Park; Page 54—Salem Witch Museum; Page 58—Old Sturbridge Village; Page 60—Commonwealth Zoological Corp./Linda Schwartz; Page 68—Commonwealth Zoological Corp./Kathleen Rutledge; Page 72—New England Aquarium; Pages 76 (top)—© Sports Action/Steve Babineau; Page 78 (top)—Glenn James/NBA Photos; Page 78 (bottom)—Noren Trotman/NBA Photos; Page 80—© Sports Action/Brian Babineau; Pages 84, 92 (both), 123—Museum of Science; Page 86 (both)—The Children's Museum; Page 88—Fayfoto/John Rich; Page 90—Boston Tea Party Ship & Museum; Page 94—L. Barry Heatherington/MIT; Page 96 (both)—© President and Fellows of Harvard College; Page 98—John F. Kennedy Library; Page 100—Courtesy Museum of Fine Arts, Boston; Page 102—Puppet Showplace Theatre; Page 110—Boston Children's Theatre; Page 112 (both)—© Justin A. Knight.

Peabody Essex Museum

East India Square
Salem, MA 01970
800-745-4054

UP TO $4.00 VALUE!

Expires 9/15/99

Buy one ticket and get one child's ticket free OR $3 off one family admission.

KIDDING AROUND® BOSTON

Old Sturbridge Village

Route 20
Sturbridge, MA 01566
508-347-3362

$7.50 VALUE!

Expires 9/15/99

Free youth admission (6–15) with each paid adult admission. Kids under six always admitted free. Not valid with other discounts. C-35

KIDDING AROUND® BOSTON

Plimoth Plantation

Exit 4 on Route 3 South
Plymouth, MA
508-746-1622

UP TO $8.00 VALUE!

Expires 9/15/99

Valid for $2 off adult admission and $1 off children's admission for up to four admissions.

KIDDING AROUND® BOSTON

Puppet Showplace Theatre

32 Station Street
Brookline Village, MA 02146
617-731-6400

TWO FOR THE PRICE OF ONE!

Expires 9/15/99

Buy one full-price ticket and receive a second ticket for the same performance free. Not valid on holiday or school vacation shows or with other discounts.

KIDDING AROUND® BOSTON

Franklin Park & Stone Zoos

1 Franklin Park Zoo
Boston, MA 02121
617-442-2002

TWO FOR THE PRICE OF ONE!

Expires 9/15/99

Valid for one free child's admission with a paying adult to Franklin Park or Stone Zoo.

KIDDING AROUND® BOSTON

New England Aquarium

Central Wharf
Boston, MA 02110
617-973-5200

$5.00 VALUE!

Expires 9/15/99

Present this coupon for one free junior admission with one paying general admission. Not valid with other discounts.

KIDDING AROUND® BOSTON

coupons coupons coupons coupons coupons coupons coupons coupons coupons coupons coupons coupons coupons coupons

Computer Museum
300 Congress Street
Boston, MA 02210
617-423-6758

$7.00! VALUE

Expires 9/15/99

www.tcm.org

Valid for 20% off the admission price for up to five guests.

(Code: TWE)

KIDDING AROUND® BOSTON

Concord Museum
200 Lexington Road
Concord, MA 01742
508-369-9609

$6.00! VALUE

Expires 9/15/99

Valid for one free adult admission with one paid child admission. Not valid with other discounts.

KIDDING AROUND® BOSTON

John F. Kennedy Library and Museum
Columbia Point
Boston, MA 02125
617-929-4523

$4.00! VALUE

Expires 9/15/99

Buy one adult admission and receive two children's admissions free.

KIDDING AROUND® BOSTON

MIT Museum
265 Massachusetts Avenue
Cambridge, MA 02139
617-253-4444

$2.00! VALUE

Expires 9/15/99

Buy one adult admission and receive two children's admissions free.

KIDDING AROUND® BOSTON

Museum of Fine Arts
465 Huntington Avenue
Boston, MA 02115
617-369-3300

$2.00! VALUE

Expires 9/15/99

Valid for $2 off one adult admission. Kids always admitted free. Excludes special exhibitions.

KIDDING AROUND® BOSTON

New Bedford Whaling Museum
18 Johnny Cake Hill
New Bedford, MA 02740
508-997-0046

$4.00! VALUE

Expires 9/15/99

Valid for $1 off admission for up to four people. Valid Monday–Friday only.

KIDDING AROUND® BOSTON